THE LIBRARY OF TRADITIONAL WISDOM

The Library of Traditional Wisdom has as its aim to present a series of works founded on Tradition, this term being defined as the transmission, over time, of permanent and universal truths, whose written sources are the revealed Scriptures as well as the writings of great spiritual masters.

This series is thus dedicated to the *Sophia Perennis* or *Religio Perennis* which is the timeless metaphysical truth underlying the diverse religions, together with its essential methodological consequences.

It is in the light of the *Sophia Perennis,* which views every religion "from within," that may be found the keys for an adequate understanding which, joined to the sense of the sacred, alone can safeguard the irreplaceable values and genuine spiritual possibilities of the great religions.

ROOTS
of the
HUMAN CONDITION

FRITHJOF SCHUON

WORLD WISDOM BOOKS

Translated from the French

First published in French as
Racines de la condition humaine
La Table Ronde
Paris, 1990

Library of Congress Cataloging-in-Publication Data

Schuon, Frithjof, 1907-
[Racines de la condition humaine. English]
Roots of the human condition /Frithjof Schuon.
p. cm.—(The Library of traditional wisdom)
Translation of: Racines de la condition humaine.
Includes bibliographical references and index.
ISBN 0-941532-11-9 : $12.00
1. Religion—Philosophy. 2. Man (Theology) 3. Theology
4. Islam—Doctrines. 5. Religions. I. Title. II. Series
BL51.S46563 1991
291.2'2—dc20 90-23459

Printed in The United States of America
For information address World Wisdom Books
P. O. Box 2682, Bloomington, Indiana 47402-2682

Contents

Preface

Roots of the Human Condition: this title suggests a perspective concerned with essentiality, hence conscious of principles, archetypes, reasons for being; conscious by virtue of intellection and not ratiocination. No doubt it is worth recalling here that in metaphysics there is no empiricism: principial knowledge cannot stem from any experience, even though experiences — scientific or other — can be the occasional causes of the intellect's intuitions. The sources of our transcendent intuitions are innate data, consubstantial with pure intelligence, but de facto "forgotten" since the "loss of Paradise"; thus principial knowledge, according to Plato, is nothing other than a "recollection," and this is a gift, most often actualized by intellectual and spiritual disciplines, *Deo juvante.*

Rationalism, taken in its broadest sense, is the very negation of Platonic anamnesis; it consists in seeking the elements of certitude in phenomena rather than in our very being. The Greeks, aside from the Sophists, were not rationalists properly speaking; it is true that Socrates rationalized the intellect by insisting on dialectic and thus on logic, but it could also be said that he intellectualized reason; there lies the ambiguity of Greek philosophy, the first aspect being represented by Aristotle, and the second by Plato, approximatively speaking. To intellectualize reason: this is an inevitable and altogether spontaneous procedure once there is the intention to express intellections that reason alone cannot attain; the difference between the Greeks and the Hindus is here a matter of degree, in the sense that Hindu thought is more "concrete" and more symbolistic than Greek thought. The truth is that it is not always possible to distinguish immediately a reasoner who accidentally has intuitions from an intuitive who in order to express himself must reason, but in practice this poses no problem, provided that the truth be saved.

Rationalism is the thought of the Cartesian "therefore," which signals a proof; this has nothing to do with the "therefore" that language demands when we intend to express a logico-ontological relationship. Instead of *cogito ergo sum,* one ought to say: *sum quia est esse,* "I am because Being is"; "because" and not "therefore." The certitude that we exist would be impossible without absolute, hence necessary, Being, which inspires both our existence and our certitude; Being and Consciousness: these are the two roots of our reality. *Vedānta* adds Beatitude, which is the ultimate content of both Consciousness and Being.

To know, to will, to love: this is man's whole nature and consequently it is his whole vocation and duty. To know totally, to will freely, to love nobly; or in other words: to know the Absolute, and ipso facto its relationships with the relative; to will what is demanded of us by virtue of this knowledge; and to love both the true and the good, and that which manifests them here below; thus to love the beautiful which leads to them. Knowledge is total or integral to the extent that its object is the most essential and thus the most real; the will is free to the extent that its aim is that which, being the most real, frees us; and love is noble by the depth of the subject as much as by the loftiness of the object; nobleness depends upon our sense of the sacred. *Amore e'l cuor gentil sono una cosa:* the mystery of love and that of knowledge coincide.

Part One

Principles and Roots

On Intelligence

Intelligence is the perception of a reality, and a fortiori the perception of the Real as such. It is ipso facto discernment between the Real and the unreal — or the less real — first in the principial, absolute or "vertical" sense, and then in the existential, relative or "horizontal" sense. More specifically, the "horizontal" or cosmic dimension is the domain of reason and of the temptation of rationalism, whereas the "vertical" or metacosmic dimension is that of the intellect, of intellection and of unitive contemplation. And let us recall that among all earthly creatures man alone possesses a vertical posture, which indicates the "vertical" potentiality of the spirit and thereby man's reason for being.[1]

It is necessary to distinguish in the human spirit between functions and aptitudes: in the first category, which is the more fundamental, we shall distinguish between discrimination and contemplation,[2] and then between analysis and

1. We must note in this context that the vertical position is also met with in certain aquatic birds, which is explained by the readily paradoxical play of Universal Possibility. In a less rigorous sense, verticality could even be attributed to all birds, in which case it would have to be recalled that birds in general manifest, hence symbolize, celestial states, although certain species, on the contrary, have a malefic yet still "supernatural" signification, by virtue of the symbolism of wings.

2. Or "conception" and "assimilation," the first function being active and as it were masculine, and the second, passive and feminine.

synthesis;[3] in the second category, we shall distinguish between an intelligence that is theoretical and another that is practical,[4] and then between one that is spontaneous and another that is reactive, or again between an intelligence that is constructive and another that is critical.[5] From an entirely different standpoint, it is necessary to distinguish between a cognitive faculty that is merely potential, another that is virtual and a third that is effective: the first pertains to all men, thus also to the most limited; the second concerns men who are uninformed but capable of learning; the third coincides with knowledge.

*

* *

It is only too evident that mental effort does not automatically give rise to the perception of the real; the most capable mind may be the vehicle of the grossest error. The paradoxical phenomenon of even a "brilliant" intelligence being the vehicle of error is explained first of all by the possibility of a mental operation that is exclusively "horizontal," hence lacking all awareness of "vertical" relationships; however, the definition "intelligence" still applies, because there is

3. In *Shingon* Buddhism, one of the two fundamental diagrams *(mandara,* from *mandala)* represents the Universe with respect to analysis or unfolding, whereas the other suggests synthesis or the root; all of which shows that the functions of the human spirit lend themselves to the most important spiritual applications.

4. Or, abstract and concrete. Both of these terms, however, present the inconvenience of being improperly used: too often, one terms "abstract" that which pertains to the principial or universal order, and "concrete" all that is phenomenal; as if God were an abstraction, and as if only phenomena were realities. In the Scholastic dispute over universals, the whole question was that of knowing what was meant by a "universal," or of knowing in what manner a principial or archetypal reality was envisaged.

5. There are other modes, such as presence of mind, cleverness, cunning, but these are of an inferior level and moreover are met with in the animal kingdom as well.

still a discernment between something essential and something secondary, or between a cause and an effect. A decisive factor in the phenomenon of "intelligent error" is plainly the intervention of an extra-intellectual element, such as sentimentality or passion; the exclusivism of "horizontality" creates a void that the irrational necessarily comes to fill. It should be noted that "horizontality" is not always the negation of the supernatural; it may also be the case of a believer whose intellectual intuition remains latent, this being precisely what constitutes the "obscure merit of faith"; in such a case one may, without absurdity, speak of devotional and moral "verticality."

Transformist evolutionism offers a patent example of "horizontality" in the domain of the natural sciences, owing to the fact that it puts a biological evolution of "ascending" degrees in place of a cosmogonic emanation of "descending" degrees.[6] Similarly, modern philosophers — mutatis mutandis — replace metaphysical causality with "physical" and empirical causalities, which no doubt demands intelligence, but one that is purely cerebral.

It is a paradoxical fact that an understanding which is equal to "vertical" truths does not always guarantee the integrity of "horizontal" intelligence or of the corresponding moral qualities; in such cases we are presented either with a unilateral development of speculative gifts to the detriment of operative gifts, or with an anomaly comprising a kind of scission of personality; but these are contingencies having nothing absolute about them in the face of the miracle of the intellect and of the truth. Nevertheless, metaphysical intelligence is integral and efficient only on condition that the speculative and operative dimensions be kept in balance.

6. We understand the term "emanation" in the Platonic sense: the starting point remains transcendent, hence unaffected, whereas in deist or naturalist emanationism the cause pertains to the same ontological order as the effect.

*

* *

Perhaps it is here worth elucidating the ambiguous phenomenon of naivety: it is above all a lack of experience combined with credulity, as is shown by the example of even the most intelligent children. Credulity can have a positive basis: it can be the attitude of a truthful man who quite naturally believes that everyone is like him; there are peoples who are credulous because they are unacquainted with lying. It thus goes without saying that naivety can be something quite relative: a man who does not know the psychology of madmen is naive in the eyes of psychiatrists, even if he is very far from being stupid. If it is necessary to be "prudent as serpents and harmless as doves,"[7] it is above all because the surroundings lay ambushes and one has to know how to defend oneself, which means that our imagination must be aware of the caprices of earthly *māyā*.

Be that as it may, if we keep to the ordinary meaning of the term, to be naive is to remain within the simplifying and materializing perspective of childhood, without thereby having to lose the instinct for "the one thing needful," which demands neither complex experiences nor a gift for abstract speculation.

We would like to reply here to the following question: has a man freed from a pernicious error thereby become more intelligent? From the standpoint of potential intelligence, no; but from the standpoint of effective intelligence, yes, certainly; for in this respect, truth equals intelligence. The

7. Which also makes one think of the "poor in spirit," who certainly are not supposed to lack mental faculties. There is the following well-known story: the fellow novices of the young Thomas Aquinas, knowing his credulity — real or apparent — called him one day to show him "a flying cow," and then mocked him because he ran to the window to see the phenomenon; he answered them: "A flying cow is less extraordinary than a lying monk."

proof is that the acceptance of a key truth entails the capacity to understand — as by a chain reaction — other truths of the same order, in addition to a multitude of subordinate applications; every comprehension illumines, every incomprehension obscures.

Contrary to naivety is luciferian, exploring, inventive intelligence, which passionately and blindly plunges into the unknown and the indefinite; it is the story of Prometheus and Icarus, and it is a suicidal curiosity.

*
* *

Intelligence gives rise not only to discernment, but also — ipso facto — to the awareness of our superiority in relation to those who do not know how to discern; contrary to what many moralists think, this awareness is not in itself a fault, for we cannot help being aware of something that exists and is perceptible to us thanks to our intelligence, precisely. It is not for nothing that objectivity is one of man's privileges.

But the same intelligence that makes us aware of a superiority, also makes us aware of the relativity of this superiority and, more than this, it makes us aware of all our limitations. This means that an essential function of intelligence is self-knowledge: hence the knowledge — positive or negative according to the aspects in view — of our own nature.

To know God, the Real in itself, the supremely Intelligible, and then to know things in the light of this knowledge, and in consequence also to know ourselves: these are the dimensions of intrinsic and integral intelligence, the only one worthy of the name, strictly speaking, since it alone is properly human.

We have said that intelligence produces, by its very essence, self-knowledge, with the virtues of humility and charity; but it may also produce, outside its essence or nature and as a consequence of a luciferian perversion, that vice of vices which is pride. Hence the ambiguity of the notion of "intelligence" in religious moralities, along with the accentuation of a humility which is expressly extra-intellectual, and for that very reason ambiguous and dangerous in its turn, since "there is no right superior to that of the Truth."

*

* *

To the question of knowing whether it is better to have intelligence or a good character, we reply: a good character. Why? Because, when this question is asked, one is never thinking of integral intelligence, which essentially implies self-knowledge; conversely, a good character always implies an element of intelligence, obviously on condition that the virtue be real and not compromised by an underlying pride, as is the case in the "zeal of bitterness." Good character is open to the truth[8] exactly as intelligence faithful to its substance opens onto virtue; we could also say that moral perfection coincides with faith, and thus could not be a social perfectionism devoid of spiritual content.

If the cognitive faculty consists in discerning between the essential and the secondary and if, by way of consequence, it implies the capacity to grasp situations and adapt to them, then he who can grasp the meaning of life and thus of death will be concretely intelligent. This means that the awareness of death ought to determine the quality of life, just as the awareness of eternal values takes precedence over temporal values. If we are asked — and we digress here — what it is that proves the reality of eternal values, we reply: among other things the very phenomenon of intelligence, which in

8. "To err is human," says Saint Jerome, and Saint Augustine adds: "but to persist in error out of passion is diabolical." Passion here coincides with pride, which in practice annuls all the virtues; similarly, error corrupts intelligence, fundamentally and setting aside the question of practical or profane matters.

fact would be inexplicable — because deprived of its reason for being — without its most fundamental or loftiest contents. There lies the entire mystery of the phenomenon of subjectivity, so strangely uncomprehended by moderns, whereas it is, precisely, an irrecusable sign of immaterial reality and of transcendence.

*

* *

The evolutionist rationalists are of the opinion that Aristotle, being the father of logic, is ipso facto the father of intelligence become at last mature and efficacious; they obviously are unaware that this flowering of a discipline of thought, while having its merits, goes more or less hand in hand with a weakening, or even an atrophy, of intellectual intuition. The angels, it is said, do not possess reason, for they have no need of reasoning; this need presupposes in fact that the spirit, no longer able to see, must "grope." It may be objected that the greatest metaphysicians, hence the greatest intellectual intuitives, made use of reasoning; no doubt, but this was only in their dialectic — intended for others — and not in their intellection as such. It is true that a reservation applies here: since intellectual intuition does not a priori encompass all aspects of the real, reasoning may have the function of indirectly provoking a "vision" of some aspect; but in this case reasoning operates merely as an occasional cause, it is not a constitutive element of the cognition. We will perhaps be told that reasoning may actualize in any thinker a suprarational intuition, which is true in principle, yet in fact it is more likely that such an intuition will not be produced, as there is nothing in the profane mentality that is predisposed thereto, to say the least.

In the preceding considerations, we do not have Aristotle in mind, we blame only those who believe that Aristotelianism represents a monopoly of intelligence, and who confuse simple logic with intelligence as such, something which Aristotle never dreamed of doing.[9] That logic can be useful or necessary for earthly man is obvious; but it is also obvious that logic is not what leads directly and indispensably to knowledge — which does not mean that illogicality is legitimate or that the suprarational coincides with the absurd. If it were objected that in mysticism and even in theology there exists a pious absurdity, we would reply that in this case absurdity is merely "functional" — somewhat as in the *koans* of Zen — and that it is necessary to examine the underlying intentions in order to do justice to the dialectic means; in this domain, there is a case for saying that "the end justifies the means."

Curiously, religious dogmatism, while stimulating intelligence through its truths which are universal in substance, also paralyzes it through its limitations; anthropomorphist theologies cannot in fact escape impasses and contradictions, because they are obliged to combine the complexity of metaphysical Reality with a personal God, hence with a single subjectivity which, as such, cannot assume that complexity.

*

* *

A few words on gnosis are called for here, since we are speaking of intelligence and since gnosis is the way of the intellect. We say "gnosis" and not "Gnosticism," for the latter is most often a heterodox mythological dogmatism, whereas intrinsic gnosis is not other than what the Hindus mean by *jnāna* and *Advaita-Vedānta*. To claim that all gnosis

9. It should be noted that India also developed a science of logic, namely the *Nyāyā* of Gautama, analyzing vicious reasonings with particular care; traces of this school are found in a number of subsequent dialecticians. This parallelism between Greece and India is explained by what we may, quite approximatively, term Aryan intellectualism, in which the hellenized Semites obviously participate.

is false because of Gnosticism, amounts to saying, by analogy, that all prophets are false because there are false prophets.

For too many people the gnostic is someone who, feeling illumined from within rather than by Revelation, takes himself to be superhuman and believes that for him everything is permissible; one will accuse of gnosis any political monster who is superstitious or who has vague interests in the occult while believing himself to be invested with a mission in the name of some aberrant philosophy. In a word, in common opinion gnosis equals "intellectual pride," as if this were not a contradiction in terms, pure intelligence coinciding precisely with objectivity, which by definition excludes all subjectivism, hence especially pride which is its least intelligent and coarsest form.

If there exists a "Gnosticist" or pseudo-gnostic satanism, there also exists an anti-gnostic satanism, and this is the comfortable and dishonest bias that sees gnosis wherever the devil is; it is to this mania — which strictly speaking pertains to the "sin against the Holy Ghost" — that may be applied Christ's injunction not to cast pearls before swine nor to give what is holy to the dogs. For if in the human order there are pearls and holiness, these are certainly to be found on the side of the intellect, which is, according to Meister Eckhart, *aliquid increatum et increabile,* hence something divine, and this is precisely what annoys and disturbs the partisans of pious superficiality and militant fanaticism.

The preceding reflections allow us to pass to a more particular subject, although pertaining to the same order of ideas. Esoterism, which coincides with gnosis, is confronted de facto with three adverse forces: quite obviously with the devil, since he is against all that is spiritual, but then also, in an altogether different way, with exoterism which, while having the right to exist, represents a limited perspective; finally, and this is particularly serious, it is confronted by the combination of the two forces just mentioned. In this last case, the attack against gnosis goes hand in hand with a reviling of religion; now this monstrous connivance would not be possible if there were not a certain imperfection in the confessional standpoint itself, which moreover is proven in its own way by the stupidities and crimes perpetrated in the name of religion; the confessions participate inevitably — or providentially if one will — in the imperfections of the human collectivities to which they are addressed in this "dark age."[10]

On the one hand, esoterism may prolong religion considered with respect to its metaphysical and mystical symbolism, but on the other hand, esoterism cannot avoid contradicting religion inasmuch as the latter is merely a limiting adaptation, for "there is no right superior to that of the truth." It is impossible to understand fully the relationship between the exoteric and esoteric aspects of a tradition without being aware of these two relationships,[11] contradictory yet anchored in the nature of things and therefore complementary.

All these considerations are justified in our general context because plenary esoterism is the way of intellection, hence of intelligence, whereas exoterism is the way of belief or faith, which cannot but affect the metaphysical speculations occurring in such surroundings. Faith, represented above all by the Semites, enjoins us to believe "in God, the Father Almighty, Creator of heaven and earth"; on the contrary, intellection, represented above all by the Aryans, reveals to us that "*Brahman* alone is real, the world is merely an appearance, and the soul is none other than *Brahman.*" This difference in perspective does not prevent faith from

10. "Why callest thou me good?" Christ said; which can be applied to the religious form, to the confessional system.

11. The sentimental combination of which resulted in a semi-esoterism that is widespread in the East, although this does not mean that a particular personal spirituality could not compensate and overcome this obstacle. Besides, if pure gnosis has to remain more or less secret in fideist surroundings, it is partly because of the rights of fideism; nonetheless, the spiritual chaos of our epoch permits or requires that the "inward" be manifested "outwardly," for "it is better that wisdom be divulged than that it be forgotten."

necessarily comprising an element of intellection, whereas intellection for its part also necessarily comprises an element of faith.

*
* *

Let us now return to the question of intelligence in general. The abuse of intelligence must not be confused with intelligence itself, as was done in classical Greece, the Renaissance, the Age of Philosophy, the Nineteenth Century and, with new and rather unpleasant modalities, in the Twentieth; the human spirit has the right to be creative only to the extent that it is contemplative, and if it has this quality, it will acknowledge that which "is" before busying itself with that which "may be."

The progressivist ideology of the Nineteenth Century believed that it could reduce the problem of the human spirit, in a certain respect at least, to the rather expeditious distinction between "civilized" and "barbarian" peoples. Now if to be intelligent is to be realistic, the Red Indians for example, with their ecological realism, were more intelligent than the chimerically industrialist Whites, and they were so not merely on the surface, but in depth. And this allows us to note that the naturism of peoples without written language is based, more often than one may be prepared to admit, on a "primordial choice" that is far from being devoid of wisdom. Instinctively distrusting the intelligence of the sorcerer's apprentice, they preferred to abstain.[12]

12. Their axioms are: if you create something — by going too far in outwardness and concretization — you become its slave; and: urban conglomerations produce both degeneracy and calamities. These convictions explain the vandalism of naturist peoples when they become conquerors, even though afterwards they cannot resist the hypnosis of urban civilizations. Judeo-Moslem iconoclasm is not unconnected with this perspective.

Be that as it may, and speaking quite generally, to the question of knowing whether mankind is effectively intelligent, one has the right to reply in the negative, in good conscience since we find ourselves in the Iron Age. On the whole, only the sages and saints are concretely intelligent;[13] they are looked upon as superhuman — rightly so from a certain point of view — whereas in fact, being realists, they are simply normal men, or primordial men, if we have in mind the spiritual conditions of the Golden Age. And this allows us to formulate, in a synthetic and almost lapidary manner, the following considerations:

Primordial man knew by himself that God is; fallen man does not know it; he must learn it. Primordial man was always aware of God; fallen man, while having learned that God is, must force himself to be aware of it always. Primordial man loved God more than the world; fallen man loves the world more than God, he must therefore practice renunciation. Primordial man saw God everywhere, he had the sense of archetypes and of essences and was not enclosed in the alternative "flesh or spirit"; fallen man sees God nowhere, he sees only the world as such, not as the manifestation of God.

Primordiality is the *fiṭrah* of the Sufis: it is essential and normative human nature, created in the image of the Creator; and for that very reason it is intelligence as such, projection of the Divine Consciousness. For "I was a hidden treasure and I wished to be known, hence I created the world;" and with it the human spirit.

13. Not the scientists who, in the final analysis, only end by destroying the world and man.

The Veil of Isis

The explorers of substance, of energy, of the indefinitely small and of the indefinitely large, proceeding from discovery to discovery and from hypothesis to hypothesis, may well plunge into the mechanism of the physical world; they will undoubtedly meet with a variety of instructive insights into the structure of the physical categories, but in fact they will never reach the end of their trajectory; the foundations of existence have something indefinite to them and will not surrender themselves. Isis is "all that has been, all that is, and all that shall be"; and "no one hath ever lifted my veil." It is useless to try to do so, all the more so in that in this order of magnitude the useless coincides with the pernicious, as is shown by the myths of Prometheus, Icarus, the Titans, and Lucifer, and as is proven to excess by the experiences of the last two centuries.[1]

Starting from the axiom that all knowledge by definition comprises a subject and an object, we shall specify the following: the subject of the knowledge of sensible phenomena is obviously a particular sensorial faculty or the combination of these faculties; the subject of the knowledge of physical principles, or of cosmic categories, is the rational

1. It should not be forgotten in this context that modern science operates with instruments — in the broadest sense — that in a traditional civilization could not exist; this means that there are kinds of knowledge that, strictly speaking, have no right to exist.

faculty; and the subject of the knowledge of metaphysical principles — and it is of this that we wish to speak — is the pure intellect and hence intellectual intuition; intuition or intellection and not discursive operation. A knowledge whose subject is not the intellect could not be metaphysical; starting from the observation of phenomena, one cannot reach a reality that only "God in us" can cause us to perceive. Three subjectivities, three modes of certitude: from the relative to the absolute.

"No one hath ever lifted my veil": it is true, in virtue of the Platonic principle that the Good tends to communicate itself, that the Goddess can consent to unveil Herself; but only in part. She does so through the phenomena of beauty and goodness, thereby allowing mortals to participate in the mystery of infinitude and in the nectar of Her beatitude; but She does not unveil her very substance, nor could She wish to do so, given the imperatives of Her nature, those of the Infinite, precisely. As we have said, this restriction concerns only the strictly individual, hence narrowly rational and "profane" subjectivity, and not that divine presence in us which is situated "on the other side" of the veil, and which coincides with the Subject as such, the only one that is; but it is certainly not this transcendent subjectivity that scientism requires and has in view.

Moreover, and this is essential: this latter subjectivity, which in reality is primary, reaches the metaphysical substance of the world starting from — or through — every positive phenomenon; there is no need for it to analyze indefinitely the physical categories in the hope of arriving at an end. Isis can lift her veil starting from an earthly beauty as well as starting from a quintessential substrate, on the assumption that it is accessible "from the outside."

One of two things: either one arrives by an objective path at what one believes to be the immanent omega of physical existence, in which case there will always remain an undeciphered element precisely because the supposed omega is objective; or else one goes beyond such an element, in which case the awareness is connected with the intellective subjectivity of man and it is no longer a question of investigation ab extra.

Unquestionably, supreme knowledge, which pertains to the absolute, can never depend intrinsically on cultural or historical contingencies; what matters to it, and what suffices, is that the world is the world and that man is man.

*

* *

When God created man in His image, He created a measure; the human perception of the world corresponds to God's creative intention.[2] Man by definition is a center, or "the center" in a given universe; not by accident, but in virtue of the very nature of Being, and this is why that which is large or small for man is large or small in the divine intention; man perceives things as they present themselves in the divine Intellect. And that is why the world of the indefinitely small, as well as the world of the indefinitely large, is as it were forbidden to man, who should not want to disproportionately enlarge the small or to disproportionately reduce the large. Man ought to feel that there is no advantage or happiness in such enterprises; and he would feel it if he had maintained a relationship with the Absolute, or if this relationship were sincere and sufficient. He who is really at peace with God is free from all unhealthy curiosity, if one may say so; he lives, like a well-guarded child, in the blessed garden of a grace that does not forsake him; the Creator knows the best place for the creature, and He knows what is good for man.

In a certain sense, the world of atoms as well as that of galaxies — to express ourselves grosso modo — is hostile to

2. According to the Koran, it was in fact man who gave all creatures their names. This innate science of the identity of things implies a priori the innate knowledge of God, and a posteriori the indirect vision of God starting from things.

human beings, and comprises for them, in principle or potentially, a climate of alienation and terror. Some people will doubtless argue that "the man of our times" is an "adult," but this is pride, even satanism, for a normal man always keeps a childlike side, as all sacred Scriptures attest by their language; if such were not the case, childhood itself would not comprise a positive aspect. Of course, a mature man ought to be "adult," but he can be so otherwise than by plunging into forbidden abysses; the spiritual victory over illusion is a matter appreciably more serious than the insensitivity of the explorers of the inhuman.

There are two points to consider in created things, namely the empirical appearance and the mechanism; now the appearance manifests the divine intention, as we have stated above; the mechanism merely operates the mode of manifestation. For example, in man's body the divine intention is expressed by its form, its deiformity,[3] its symbolism and its beauty; the mechanism is its anatomy and vital functioning. The modern mentality, having always a scientific and "iconoclastic" tendency, tends to overaccentuate the mechanism to the detriment of the creative intention, and does so on all levels, psychological as well as physical; the result is a jaded and "demystified" mentality that is no longer "impressed" by anything. By forgetting the divine intention — which nonetheless is apparent a priori — one ends in an emptiness devoid of all reference points and meaning, and in a mentality of nihilism and despair, if not of careless and brutal materialism. In the face of this deviation it is the child who is right when he believes that the blue sky above us is Paradise.

That there are sciences, including physical sciences, is in man's nature because it is in the nature of things; but it is quite as much in the nature of things that man is unable to

3. We should specify: total or integral deiformity, for in animals too there is — or can be — a deiformity, but it is partial; similarly for plants, minerals, elements and other orders of phenomena.

unveil Isis and that he must not try to do so. Human science has limits of principle; what in traditional civilizations prevents man from overstepping these limits is his relationship with God, with all the consequences that this relationship implies.[4]

*
* *

One point that certain physicists do not seem to understand is that the mechanism of the world can be neither purely deterministic nor a fortiori purely arbitrary. In reality, the universe is a veil woven of necessity and freedom, of mathematical rigor and musical play; every phenomenon participates in these two principles, which amounts to saying that everything is situated in two apparently divergent but at bottom concordant dimensions, exactly as the dimensions of space are concordant while giving rise to divergent appearances that are irreconcilable from the standpoint of a planimetric view of objects.[5]

Another point that moderns do not grasp, is that there is no reason for necessarily seeking the cause of a phenomenon on the plane where it is produced, and that on the contrary one has to consider the possibility of a non-material cause, above all when it is a question of a phenomenon

4. Although a believer, Pasteur is supposed to have said that when entering his laboratory he left God outside; be that as it may, this plainly shows the false realism of scientists, while at the same time — in a quite different respect — it demonstrates the inferiority complex of those who are still believers towards the apparently victorious rationalists.

5. Let us take the example of the human body: its principial form, which cannot be other than what it is, stems from the Absolute and from necessity, whereas its actual form — a particular body, and not the body as such — which gives rise to innumerable variations, stems from the Infinite and from freedom. Its principial form is as it were mathematical, it is measurable; on the contrary, its actual form is as it were musical, its beauty is unfathomable. Anatomy has its limits, beauty does not; but beauty can be relative, whereas anatomy cannot.

whose beginning is unknown a priori, and unknowable materially, as is the origin of living beings. Transformist evolutionism is the classical example of the bias that invents "horizontal" causes because one does not wish to admit a "vertical" dimension: one seeks to extort from the physical plane a cause that it cannot furnish and that is necessarily situated above matter.

Even within the order of physical causes, one has to take into account the simultaneous presence of the immanent metaphysical Cause: if a seed is the immediate cause of a plant, it is because the divine archetype intervenes in the physical causality. Geometrically speaking, causes can be situated on the "concentric circles" that constitute the Universe, but other causes — and with all the more reason the First Cause — are situated at the Center and act through the radii emanating from it. The divine Intellect contains the archetypes of creation, and it is starting from this Cause — or from this causal system — at a given cyclic "moment" of the cosmogonic process, that the "ideas" are "incarnated" which will be manifested in the form of contingent creatures.

We do not ask physicists to be content with an anthropomorphic and naive creationism; but at least it would be logical on their part — since they aim at a total and flawless science — to try to understand the traditional onto-cosmological doctrines, especially the Hindu doctrine of the "envelopes *(kosha)* of the Self *(Ātmā)*"; a doctrine that, precisely, presents the Universe as a system of circles proceeding from the Center-Principle to that extreme limit which for us is matter. For human science does not derive solely from the need to know and to register; more profoundly its origin is the thirst for the essential; now the sense of essentiality attracts us toward shores other than those of the limited plane of physical phenomena alone.

*
* *

As regards the illegitimacy of any attempt to overstep the limits imposed by the mystery of Isis, it could be objected that metaphysics is also such an attempt. This argument applies to profane philosophy, but not to the *scientia sacra* by which Isis Herself consents to lift a veil, without however withdrawing it to the point of leaving no mystery. The goal of the profane thinkers on the contrary is to propose to the intelligence only what is rationally verifiable and to "free" thought from all transcendence; the intention is to "demystify" the universe by explaining it once and for all; thus rationalistic language wishes to exhaust the knowable to the last drop. Thought is then all that language expresses and nothing more.

To attempt to raise the veil of Isis is not to explain God and the world, the Principle and its Manifestation, while knowing that it is impossible to exhaust the mystery of the Real; it is rather to wish to discover and to explain all of Possibility with the intention of unveiling it totally. As we have specified more than once in our writings, metaphysics intends to furnish dialectically only reference points. Pedants will blame it for being incomplete, for not taking into account this or that; but articulated metaphysics is necessarily incomplete, precisely because it is articulated; nevertheless it offers — and this is its entire reason for being — a system of perfectly sufficient keys, through a language that cannot be other than indicative and elliptical. If, throughout the course of history, one such doctrine is added to other analogous doctrines, it is not — except exceptionally and for reasons of accentuation — because the preceding doctrines were deemed erroneous, but simply because a new formulation was deemed opportune — to begin with by Heaven itself which presides over the manifestations of the Spirit.

No one shall raise the veil of Isis, says the Egyptian tradition; nevertheless, it may happen not only that the Goddess Herself lifts her veil, but even that the veil disappears altogether; this Mystery, which appears to contradict what we have said before, is not however situated on the same level as the gestures of mercy and it is not addressed to the individual as such. The nudity of Isis pertains to the "heart," or to the immanent Self; instead of speaking of "unveiling," another image could be chosen and it could be said that the Goddess takes the soul under Her veil, ab intra; this, in Sufic terms, is "knowledge through *Allāh,*" in which it is less the intelligence that perceives God than it is God who perceives Himself in the intelligence. What is involved, therefore, is that Intellect which Meister Eckhart termed "that something in the soul *(aliquid est in anima)* which is uncreated and uncreatable," and which belongs to us because we belong to it; "the kingdom of God is within you." The inward dimension is unitive by its nature because it is the projection of the divine Self, transcendent in itself but rendered immanent in virtue of the ontological homogeneity of the Universe.

*
* *

As the veil of Isis is found within us as well as above us, certain considerations on the notions of objectivity and subjectivity can find a place here. The meaning of these two notions is either philosophical or psychological, according to whether they correspond either to definitions or to attitudes: thus we may consider each of these ideas either in an objective sense, having in view their suchness, or in a subjective sense, relating to our awareness. To consider subjectivity objectively is to define it as a phenomenon; to consider objectivity subjectively is to see it as a quality of the subject, as absence of subjectivism, precisely, and thus as the adequate perception of "external" reality.

If the fundamental quality of the object is reality — and objective things are precious to the extent that they manifest the absolute Real or come close to it in various modes and in different degrees — the fundamental quality of the subject will be intelligence, the intellect, pure intellection and hence metaphysical certitude; intellection being as exact and unquestionable as the objective reality that surrounds us.

Furthermore: if in the ordinary usage of the words "subjectivity" means a predominance of sentimentality which engenders bias, one could as well mean by "objectivity" the abusive preoccupation — to the detriment of inward values — with the things of the external world, something which nobody has dreamt of doing. In other words: when subjectivity is opposed to objectivity, the latter appears to be superior and normative; when, however, inwardness is opposed to outwardness, in the moral or spiritual sense of the terms, it is inwardness that has priority.

Obviously, subject and object form a complementarity that in itself is neutral and not an alternative comprising an opposition; on the other hand however, the subject as well as the object do comprise such an alternative or quasi-Zoroastrian bipolarity, namely: for the objective pole, Being and matter, and for the subjective pole, immanent divine Consciousness and the ego, or the Self and the "I".[6] The great perversion is to tend towards matter and towards the ego, thereby drawing away from the immanent as well as transcendent divine Principle; this is materialism on the one hand, and egoism or individualism on the other, both of which can be either theoretical or practical, that is, either philosophical or vital.

There is a "veil of Isis" on the side of the subject as well as on the side of the object: purely rational thought — cut-off from its intellective roots — cannot violate the mysteries of the Absolute-Object, any more than the empirical ego — it too separated from its substance — can violate the mysteries of the Absolute-Subject; "mystery" is that which remains inaccessible to a fragmentary consciousness. In other words:

6. The lower limits are: for the hierarchy of objective realities, the most solidified, opaque and heavy matter; for subjective realities, the most outward consciousness, namely the sensorial faculties.

the veil of the Goddess hides at one and the same time that which is too "lofty" and that which is too "deep" — or too divinely "other" and too divinely "oneself" — for minds accustomed to stopping halfway, to perceiving only contingencies, and to being only a contingency.

In the final analysis, the Isis hidden behind her veil is none other than Divine Reality in which the objective and the subjective coincide; and the veil is none other than the cosmogonic projection by which this Reality is bipolarized and gives rise to that play of innumerable mirrors that is the Universe; Isis is *Ātmā,* the veil is *Māyā.*

Problems of Space-Time

There is no doubt that integral — not merely elementary — physics cannot do without the lights of metaphysics; one of the most patent proofs of this is the fact that the principle of relativity categorically demands the concurrence of the principle of absoluteness, on pain of giving rise to a chaotic and as it were "headless" and atheistic cosmology. "The doctrine of unity is unique," say the Sufis; in a logically analogous manner it could be said, as regards the Einsteinian theory, that the doctrine of relativity is relative.

The principle of relativity relates to cosmic measures in their contingency or their "accidentality"; the principle of absoluteness on the contrary takes into account the manifestations of the absolute in the relative; it is the whole difference between the mechanism of manifestation and the symbol-message which is its content and its reason for being. On the one hand, the position of the "motionless center" proper to the sun is relative because there are other fixed stars — hence other "centers" — and because the sun with its planetary system is itself in motion; but on the other hand, and this is essential, the solar body is really situated at the center, not merely because the planets surround it, but also, metaphysically speaking, because its reason for being is to physically manifest *Ātmā* in *Māyā*. The proof of this position or function is not only the revolution of the planets, but also — and a priori — the mass and luminosity of the sun, its majesty if one will. In other words, the principle of absoluteness is always manifested by a phenomenon of eminence, by a relationship of determinant to determined, of center to periphery, precisely; and this relationship, quite obviously, is irreversible.[1] A remark is called for here: to say that the sun is situated at the center does not necessarily mean that it is thus situated in a mathematically exact fashion; doubtless, the other fixed stars are much too far to be able to influence distances within the solar system, and it is perhaps impossible to explain the real cause of the irregularity in question. Be that as it may, the ontological cause could well be the gap between the divine archetype and its physical manifestation, a gap which however is not necessarily manifested in all orders; it is manifested to the extent required by All-Possibility, and in a manner determined by it.

All this represents an application of the principle of the "relatively absolute": strictly speaking, there is only one Center — "Why callest thou me good?" Christ said — which is God, the supreme Principle; but the phenomenon "center" nonetheless exists in the spatial universe, otherwise we would have neither the notion nor the word for it; the divine Center is necessarily reflected diversely in creation which by definition is the mirror of the Creator. Relativity is inconceivable without traces of absoluteness; to say *Māyā*, is to say presence of *Ātmā*. Wherever God is reflected, there is a center, physically as well as metaphysically; now God is reflected in and by the sun, that is to say His "presence" in the sun is eminently more direct than His presence in the planets; certainly "God is everywhere," but this immanence could not abolish the hierarchy of the degrees of presence. If there were no center, space would not be space.

1. The case of double or twin stars represents, not the relationship "center-periphery", but the archetype of the sexual dance, that of *Purusha* and *Prakriti*. The immanence and invisibility of the center is so to speak the reason for being of the reciprocal movement of the two partners.

In a certain sense, the principle of absoluteness means that things are what they seem to be; the principle of relativity means on the contrary that they are other than what they appear to be. And it is precisely in virtue of the principle of absoluteness that the perspective of Ptolemy, that of humanly natural appearances, is legitimate and efficacious in its order and therefore concretely symbolic.[2] Moreover, starting from the idea that it is Copernicus who is materially right and that the geocentrists do not grant the sun its due, let us not forget that their perspective also comprises an element of heliocentrism since they admit the primacy of the solar body, something which is patently proven by all the mythologies and no less so by astrology.[3]

Also supporting our thesis of the irreversibility of the relationship sun-planets, or center-periphery, is the almost universal cult of the sun: the Sun Dance of the American Indians, for example, refers to a spiritual influence that the solar body can really communicate; here it is a question not of an arbitrarily imagined symbol, but of a true cosmic sacrament, hence of a power deriving from a mode of divine immanence.

*

* *

To speak of the enigmas of space is to imply those of time: obviously, the phenomenon of physical movement is at once spatial and temporal, and it is precisely this connection that the Einsteinian theory of relativity has in view. If there is

2. Thus it is necessary to distinguish between an appearance of this order and an accidental optical illusion: a mirage in the desert does not have the same basis nor consequently the same "rights" as the apparent course of the sun.

3. A marginal remark: the fact that modern heliocentrism coincides with the collapse of an ancient wisdom and the flowering of an increasingly scientistic and atheistic "humanism," is independent of heliocentrism as such, which could have given rise to a spiritual cosmology at least as valid as the Ptolemaic system.

something absolute in the spatial condition, the same holds true for the temporal condition: what the point or the center is to the former, the moment or the present — or the origin — is to the latter.

Assuming that the origin of the physical universe was a cosmogonic "explosion",[4] there will be no difficulty in also assuming that it is the supernatural place of the explosion that remains the center of space; the universe will then have the form of an expanding spherical shell situated between two voids, one "interior" and one "exterior". The divine "event" was like the sudden crystallization of a supersaturated chemical solution, following upon the "overfull" existentiating tendency of Being; the explosion coinciding with the origin of time, which finally will be "reabsorbed" in the apocatastasis or *mahāprālaya.*[5] And it is after the initial creative "Be!" that the creative "incarnations" were able to arise, in successive waves, at once by "emanation" and by creation *ex nihilo,* and not starting from a pre-existing substance.[6]

Time essentially comprises cycles — hence a rhythm — with summit-phases corresponding to that which in space is central and indicates absoluteness; or again, spatial extension expresses the Infinite in static mode, whereas temporal extension expresses it in dynamic mode; similarly, mutatis mutandis, for the point and the instant, or for the center and the present. All these considerations indicate in their way that an integral physics cannot be dissociated from metaphysics,[7] the science of the Absolute, precisely.

4. The "big bang," in the jargon of certain Anglo-Saxon scientists.

5. The return to the "Night of *Brahma*"; final reintegration.

6. The creation of Adam "from earth" implies on the one hand that this earth was created *ex nihilo,* and on the other that the human phenomenon is totally — and supernaturally — independent of this substance, which could not produce anything.

7. As is proven for example by the divergence between the partisans of determinism and those of accidentalism, not to mention the impasses of biology, which partly stem from this false alternative.

Mahāshakti

The term *shakti* means fundamentally the efficient energy of the Supreme Principle envisaged in itself or at a given ontological degree. For the Principle, or let us say the metacosmic Order, comprises degrees and modes in virtue of Universal Relativity, *Māyā,* in which it reverberates.

In the domain of the spiritual life, the same term *shakti* signifies the celestial energy that allows man to enter into contact with the Divinity, by means of the appropriate rites and on the basis of a traditional system. Essentially, this divine *Shakti* aids and attracts: She aids as "Mother," and attracts as "Virgin"; Her aid descends upon us from Heaven, whereas Her attraction raises us towards Heaven. This is to say that the *Shakti,* as *pontifex,* on the one hand confers a second birth, and on the other offers liberating graces.

In the Absolute, the *Shakti* is the aspect of Infinitude that coincides with All-Possibility and gives rise to *Māyā,* the universal and efficient *Shakti.* Infinitude is "Beatitude," *Ānanda,* which combines in *Ātmā* with *Sat,* "Being" or "Power",[1] and with *Chit,* "Consciousness" or "Knowledge." We could also say that the pole *Ānanda*

1. "Being," and likewise "Existence," is "Power" by definition; in the physical order, mass implies energy; all matter comprises a potential force.

results from the poles *Sat* and *Chit,* just as union or experience results from the poles object and subject; it is from this resultant that arises universal Unfolding — the creative *Māyā* with its innumerable possibilities rendered effective.

Certain objections should perhaps be anticipated here: it could in fact be asserted that *Māyā* has no cause since *Brahman* or *Ātmā* could not be the cause of anything; but this transcendent independence in no way prevents *Māyā* from being in another connection, or from another angle of vision, the effect of the Infinitude of *Ātmā,* otherwise *Māyā* would be a second Absolute. It could also be objected that the supreme Principle has no parts and that the three aspects mentioned could not constitute it, which is true but is nonetheless a way of playing with words; in reality, each of the three aspects of *Ātmā* is the Absolute and each contains the other two in an indistinct, and as it were potential, fashion; we are here at the limit of the expressible.

We have said that *Shakti* equals energy; perhaps it is not going too far to say that energy comprises essentially two poles or functions — and we are thinking here a priori of physical energy — notably, explosiveness and attractiveness, and that all the other modes, such as the rotation of a body on its axis or the revolution of one body around another, are simply effects of the two fundamental powers mentioned; both of which comprise moreover three modes, namely potentiality, virtuality and effectiveness; these modes concern explosiveness in a more immediately understandable way than attractiveness. It is in an analogous manner — mutatis mutandis — that *Māyā* "breathes," or "dances," or "weaves" the Universe; not merely the physical world, but all of *Ātmā*'s "envelopes." A priori, everything in the movement of the macrocosm, and no less so of the microcosms, is projection and attraction, each of these two principles being conceivable in either a manifesting or reintegrating sense. God is a "center" in respect of His absoluteness, and a "space" in respect of His infinitude; similarly, the world is a "center" from the point of view of its existential "weight," and a "space" from the point of view of its indefiniteness.

In the movement of heavenly bodies there are two enigmas — to which we have already alluded — namely the rotation of a body on its axis and the revolution of that body around another body; symbolically speaking, the rotation may refer to the heart and hence to the immanent Self — to *Ātmā* "contained" in *jīvātmā* — whereas the revolution will refer to Being, thus to the transcendent Principle, to *Ātmā* or *Ishvara* considered in itself. Thus, the axis of the planet corresponds — in the human microcosm — to the Heart-Intellect, and the sun corresponds — in the macrocosm — to the Divine Principle. This analogy cannot but manifest an ontological causality, given that a direct or intrinsic symbol prolongs concretely and in its own way that which it symbolizes. And to say movement, is to say energy, and consequently, *Shakti.*

As immanent and latent liberating power — or as potentiality of liberation — the *Shakti* is called *Kundalinī,* "Coiled-up," because it is compared to a sleeping snake; its awakening in the human microcosm is effected thanks to the yogic practices of tantrism. This means, from the standpoint of the nature of things or of universal spirituality, that the cosmic energy which liberates us is part of our very being, notwithstanding the graces that the *Shakti* confers upon us, through mercy, "from without" and but for which there can be no Path. In any case, just as *Mahāshakti* or *Parashakti* — the "supreme productive Energy" — equals the feminine aspect of *Brahman* or *Ātmā,* so the *Kundalinī* gives rise to a divinification that makes it the equal of the creative *Māyā.*

*

* *

The Hindu tradition teaches us that at the summit of cosmic Manifestation, thus in its still divine sector,[2] the Femininity-Principle is the trinity Sarasvati-Lakshmi-Parvati, facing the masculine trinity Brahma-Vishnu-Shiva. Sarasvati is the genius of Wisdom; Lakshmi, of Goodness, Beauty, Happiness; and Parvati, in her terrible aspect at any rate — in which case she is Durga or Kali — is the genius of Rigor, hence of divine chastisement.[3] To properly grasp the meaning of this mystery, it is important not to lose sight of its ontological structure the outline of which is as follows.

All-Possibility implies not only Beatitude, Plenitude, inexhaustible Richness, but also Overflowing or Projection and, as a result of the latter, Remoteness and Impoverishment. To the extent that the manifesting or cosmogonic Overflowing moves away from its divine Source, it suffers the lot of all radiation, in the sense that its rays grow fainter as they proceed, and it is here that the mystery of evil intervenes: the cosmogonic ray tends to be perverted in the final analysis, which is to say that it becomes luciferian and tends to make itself God; whence the divine reaction of the terrible and vengeful *Shakti,* Kali the "Black One."[4] Here one has to recall the doctrine of the three *gunas,* the three cosmic tendencies resulting from the universal Substance, *Prakriti:*[5] they are, firstly *sattva,* the luminous and ascendant tendency; secondly *rajas,* the fiery, horizontal and expansive tendency; thirdly *tamas,* which is obscure and descendant. Now the

2. Divine because "celestial" and not "terrestrial"; or let us say: beyond the *samsāra* — beyond "transmigration" — but nonetheless included in creation.

3. Parvati comprises two opposing aspects, like Shiva who personifies at once asceticism and eroticism; a paradox the key of which might be ancient Dravidian mythology.

4. To whom certain *shaktas* in former times vowed a bloody cult in order to appease her, or to exhaust the reparatory possibilities required by her.

5. The *Shakti* of *Purusha,* the Divine creative Intellect; *Purusha* and *Prakriti* being the two poles of *Ishvara,* of the creative, revealing, rewarding and judging Being; thus of the personal God.

terrible *Shakti,* Durga or Kali, corresponds to *tamas,* not because She herself could be evil — holy wrath is in itself a good — but because She is the divine reaction to what is evil, namely the luciferianism of the world; like Shiva Her spouse, She is the genius of transformation and destruction, or rather She participates in this function in an efficient manner. It could also be said that Durga presides with Shiva over the temporal condition and the evanescence of things, whereas Lakshmi presides over the spatial condition and conservation.

Let us summarize: in projecting Itself in *Māyā,* the Principle manifests Itself, but at the same time, in virtue of the cosmogonic distancing, it tends to make Itself "other than Itself," whence the evil in the world and the intervention of the terrible *Shakti* as a consequence. All this is so because All-Possibility cannot exclude the apparent negation of necessary Being.

A priori, Lakshmi is the goddess of beauty and happiness; as Mahalakshmi, the supreme Lakshmi, she is the fountain of all blessings; she obliges Vishnu to forgive men their weaknesses and their sins, as this formulation attests: "As Father, Vishnu is the Judge; as Mother (as Lakshmi) He is the Forgiver."[6] According to the advaitists, it is only by the grace of *Mahāshakti* — the Supreme *Shakti* — that man can transcend the cosmic *Māyā* and thereby obtain the realization of the "One without a second," the *Advaita,* precisely.[7]

6. Shankaracharya: "I implore thee (O Lakshmi) to regard me with thine eyes of grace, as in passing, and to me that will suffice to obtain thy flood of favors, O my Mother." Let us add that the worship of the *Shakti* was instituted by Shankara in his monasteries, which is all the more remarkable in that the *Advaita-Vedānta* proceeds by elimination, whereas the shaktic method proceeds on the contrary by sublimation.

7. Let us mention here the *shakti* as *dākinī:* the various *dākinīs* represent all possible aspects of *Māyā,* from the celestial down to the infernal; always nude and dancing, they may be malefic and bloody furies as well as protecting angels. The supreme *Dākinī* coincides with the *Bodhi,* the

Quite clearly, shaktism has a universal significance; what the mediatrix *Shakti* is for the Hindus, Isis was for the Egyptians. Apuleius reports this Egyptian prayer: "Verily, Thou art the holy and eternal savior of mankind, always ready to aid mortals; and Thou bringest the sweet love of a mother to the trials of the unfortunate." And a sanctuary of Isis in Rome bears the following inscription: "Thou, Isis, Thou art the salvation of thy worshipers."

*

* *

For obvious reasons, there is a certain relationship between the idea of *Shakti* and tantrism; as for the latter, it is important to stress that, far from being a gratuitous hedonism, it has, on the contrary, exigencies lacking which it could not constitute a spiritual method. First of all, tantrism presupposes the intuition of the metaphysical transparency of phenomena and thus the sense of archetypal realities; on this basis, it can realize the integration of natural and normal, hence legitimate, pleasures into the Path towards the archetypes and the Sovereign Good. It operates essentially with beauty, which is objective, and with pleasure, which is subjective; visual, auditive or mental beauty, that is, forms, sounds and words; and the enjoyment of smell, taste and touch, for even the experience of a sip of fresh water can evoke a cosmic and celestial analogy, which amounts to saying that it is not only privation that can have a spiritual value, despite the partisans of exclusive asceticism. Once again, the integration of the agreeable into spirituality is not gratuitous and could not be: on the one hand, the interiorizing experience of beauty presupposes nobleness of soul, which is no small matter, and on the other hand, the analogous experience of sensorial pleasure

"Illumination," with whom the devotee must unite in a quasi-"sexual" manner — that is, existentially with the heart — in order to be saved from the round of existences.

demands temperance, hence a sober character that does not admit of any excess. In the case of beauty, the complementary moral condition is analogous to the content, for only a beautiful soul has the right to a beautiful experience; whereas in the case of common pleasure — like eating and drinking, for example -- the moral condition is opposed to its content; for one can only enjoy legitimately when one knows how to sacrifice. There is no Path outside truth and virtue, whatever the appearances may be from the standpoint of formalistic and conventional moralism; what has to be stressed here, is that the tantric or shaktic perspective is based, not on rules dictated by a given social opportuneness, but on the nature of things. This nature is of divine substance and is revealed only to him who knows how to see things divinely, with the eyes of primordial man.[8]

Some clarifications concerning tantric or shaktic amoralism are called for here. The fundamental idea — which is not responsible for any subsequent deviations — is that only inward or interiorizing action is perfect, and not actions, however good they may be, that are situated outwardly and are unable to leave outwardness; hence the apparently immoral substitution of the alternative "inwardness or outwardness" for the moral alternative "good or evil." But it is not enough for the act to be inward, it must also be objectively directed towards the Absolute and subjectively free of all selfish motivation; it must combine transcendence and immanence, for in perfect inwardness, in the

8. The Christian alternative between the "flesh" and the "spirit" allows us to recall here that corporeality is not something bad in itself, despite a relative disgrace attached to it owing to the "fall." According to a teaching of the Kabalah — noted by the theosophist Oetinger and again by Schelling — the corporeal state is the terminal point of the progressive self-revelation of God; it is thus a perfection, not an imperfection. Note that the tenth and last *sephira* in this process is a feminine hypostasis, the "Maiden," thus an aspect of *Mahāshakti;* and so too — in Judaism — is the *schekhina,* the divine Presence.

"depths of the heart" which is the "kingdom of God," the subject as well as the object transcend the created order, hence the world and the ego respectively. All this enables one to understand such Sufic sayings as the following: "All is accursed in the world, save the remembrance of God"; and "the good actions of the profane *(awwām)* are the bad actions of the sages" *('ārifūn)*. That is why the Sufis appreciate, not a priori religious action accomplished in view of personal salvation, but the action coinciding with a disinterested but liberating awareness of the supreme Reality; in this context, religious actions merely play the part of adjuvants, which are in fact indispensable in most cases.[9] Be that as it may, one will understand what is meant when Islamic doctrine teaches that the prophets — we have in mind above all David, Solomon and Muhammad — are exempt from sin; although not from extrinsic and accidental, hence purely "outward" errors.

All these considerations do not in the least mean that asceticism is not a fully valid method; what has to be understood is that, from the standpoint of total truth, exclusive asceticism is not the only path possible, and also that the path of "abstraction" or elimination can be combined with that of "analogy" or sublimation. From the standpoint of this latter perspective, we would like to broach the following dimension: in Hindu spirituality there is a symbolical topography of the divine body; thus Shankara, who was an ascetic — but without narrow-mindedness — expresses himself in these terms: "O Mother! May we be relieved from all our sorrows by thy breasts, from which milk always flows and at

9. Nothing is more absurd than to affirm that the search for salvation is "selfish"; a priori, it is even man's duty, yet from the standpoint of the metaphysical consciousness of our nature, it is nonetheless a limitation, at least to the extent that it is exclusive. Vivekananda wanted one to be interested only in the salvation of others, which is nonsense, for only he who saves himself can save others; and to save others is to show them how to save oneself, *Deo juvante.*

which you suckle both Skanda and Ganesha, your sons!" Now the first is the god of war, and the second, the god of knowledge; and this means that *Mahāshakti* offers spiritual nourishment to *kshatriyas* as well as to *brahmanas.*[10]

In connection with the mystery of inwardness we have just spoken about, we should perhaps mention here the power of the *mantra,* of the word in its "uncreated" essence — thus a priori inward or cardiac — and interiorizing from the standpoint of the outward ego. The *mantra* is a revealed substitute of the primordial sound; purifying and saving, it is a manifestation of the *Shakti* as power of union.

*

* *

In Northern Buddhism, the shaktic principle is manifested by the goddess Kwan-Yin as well as by Tara.[11] Kwan-Yin — the Kannon of Japanese Buddhism — stems from the *bodhisattva* Avalokiteshvara, supreme genius of Mercy; this quality or function explains the feminization of the hypostasis. As for Tara, she is derived from *Prajnāpāramitā,* "Transcendent Wisdom"; she is "Mother of all the Buddhas"

10. Other examples drawn from the same hymn — entitled "Inundation of the Divine Splendor" *(Saundarya Lahari)* — are the following: "O Banner and Victory of the King of the Mountain (Shiva)! We have not the shadow of a doubt that thy two breasts are pitchers made of rubies and full of *amrita,* the drink of immortality! . . . O Daughter of the Mountain Indescribable and unique is the glory of thy navel, which in truth is a whirlpool on the surface of the river Ganges . . . and which is the cavity where the invincible fire of Kama Deva burns, the god of love who shoots arrows made of flowers!" — The *Srimad Bhagavatam* contains analogous symbolisms describing the body of Vishnu.

11. We are using here the word "goddess" in a symbolic and approximative, or if one wishes, practical fashion, given that Buddhism excludes the idea of a personal divinity. As for the *bodhisattvas,* they correspond on the one hand to the archangels and on the other — more ordinarily and a priori — to the great saints who save souls and afterwards enter into the celestial "iconostasis."

and "Savioress," hence *Shakti*. In the same way, Mary has been qualified as the "Mother of all the Prophets" and as "Co-Redemptress"; not to mention the epithet — actually highly elliptical — of "Mother of God."

This last example shows us that the *Shakti* can be a human person, an earthly and a posteriori heavenly woman; other examples, belonging to the Hindu world are Sita and Radha, who are sometimes invoked together with Rama and Krishna, whence the names Sitaram and Radhakrishna. In Buddhism one has to mention, aside from the *bodhisattvas*, the great figure of Maya, the mother of the Buddha, whom the *Buddhacharita* of Ashvagosha describes thus: "He (the king Shakya) had a queen named Maya, as if to say that she was free of all illusion *(māyā)*; a splendor proceeding from his splendor, like the magnificence of the sun free of all darkening influence; a queen supreme amongst the assembly of all queens. She was like a mother to her subjects . . . and she was the most eminent of the goddesses of the entire world. But having contemplated the great glory of her newborn (the Buddha) . . . queen Maya could not bear the joy he brought her; and so as not to die from it, she ascended to Heaven." Thus it is that the Mother of the Buddha, like the Mother of Christ, has a double message: her own nature and her child; the two miracles being powers of ascension and of liberation. The first of these messages is multiple and perpetual, it is an inexhaustible rain of blessings; the second is unique and historical, it is the divine maternity.[12]

The question could be asked whether human personifications of the *Shakti* occur in every religion; this could be affirmed of the more or less secondary manifestations, but not of the supreme manifestations such as those just mentioned. In the Christian world, one of the most eminent

12. In mahayanic Buddhism, we encounter also the "white Tara" and the "green Tara," both princesses married to the Tibetan king who introduced Buddhism into his country; they incarnate two different and complementary modes of celestial favors.

examples of the secondary degree is Saint Mary Magdalene, who combines the principles of Eve and Mary, which implies, as far as her personality is concerned, a certain dimension of cosmic mystery; spiritually characteristic are also her solitude, her nudity and levitation by the angels.

Islam, in the Koran, recognizes a supreme eminence in Mary; Shiism seems to attribute it also to Fatimah — daughter of the Prophet and mother of all the sharifs — or even to her alone for reasons deriving from a very particular soteriology. However that may be, there is nothing astonishing in that Islam, given its most rigorous monotheistic perspective, should be little inclined to stress a case of "human divinity," although it may do so occasionally in an indirect or implicit manner.

*
* *

According to the Koran, the names *Allāh* and *Raḥmān* are quasi-equivalent: "Call Him *Allāh* or call Him *Raḥmān*, to Him belong the most beautiful names"; which indicates the as it were shaktic character of the name *Raḥmān*. The name *Raḥīm*, "Merciful," in a way prolongs the name *Raḥmān*, "Clement"; it prolongs it in view of the creatures, and in this sense it is taught that *Allāh*, who is *Raḥmān* in His Substance, is *Raḥīm* in relation to creation, or "since" creation. The great *Shakti* in Islam is the *Raḥmah:* it is the Goodness, Beauty and Beatitude of God.[13]

There are moreover some more specific forms of the *Shakti*, such as the *Sakīnah*, the "appeasement" or the "sweetness," and the *Barakah*, the "benediction" or the "irradiation of sanctity," or again the "protective energy";

13. Note that in Arabic — and the case is analogous in Hebrew — the word *raḥmah* is derived from the root *raḥim*, a word signifying "womb," and this corroborates the interpretation of the *Raḥmah* as divine Femininity, thus as *Mahāshakti*.

all of which constitute so many images of the celestial Femininity, of the beneficent and saving *Shakti.*

From quite another point of view, it could be said that the shaktic perspective is manifested in Islam by the sacral promotion of sexuality;[14] this character puts Islam consciously and abruptly in opposition to the exclusively sacrificial and ascetic perspective of Christianity, but brings it nearer to shaktism and tantrism, at least in the relationship under consideration.[15] According to a *ḥadīth,* "marriage is half the religion"; that is to say — by analogy — that the *Shakti* is the "prolongation" of the Divine Principle; *Māyā* "prolongs" *Ātmā.* To know woman — insists Ibn 'Arabi — is to know oneself; and "Whoso knoweth his soul, knoweth his Lord." Certainly, the human soul is one, but the sexual polarity splits it, to a certain extent; now knowledge of the Absolute requires the primordial totality of the soul, for which sexual union is in principle the natural and immediate support, although obviously this totality can be realized outside the erotic perspective, as each of the sexes comprises the potentiality of the other; the human soul being one, precisely.

According to Ibn 'Arabi, *Hiya,* "She," is a divine Name like *Huwa,* "He"; but it does not follow that the word *Huwa* is limited, for God is indivisible, and to say "He" is to say "She." It is however true that *Dhāt,* the divine "Essence," is a feminine word which — like the word *Ḥaqīqah* — can refer to the superior aspect of femininity: according to this way of seeing things, which is precisely that of Hindu shaktism, femininity is what surpasses the formal, the finite, the outward; it is synonymous with indetermination, illimitation, mystery, and thus evokes the "Spirit which giveth life" in

14. This even is indicated, quite paradoxically, by the veiling of women, which suggests mystery and sacralization.

15. This does not mean that Christianity does not also comprise a quasi-tantric dimension, namely chivalry, characterized by the cult of the "lady" and no less by a particular devotion for the Virgin.

relation to the "letter which killeth." That is to say that femininity in the superior sense comprises a liquefying, interiorizing, liberating power: it liberates from sterile hardnesses, from the dispersing outwardness of limiting and compressing forms. On the one hand, one can oppose feminine sentimentality to masculine rationality — on the whole and without forgetting the relativity of things — but on the other hand, one also opposes to the reasoning of men the intuition of women; now it is this gift of intuition, in superior women above all, that explains and justifies in large part the mystical promotion of the feminine element; it is consequently in this sense that the *Ḥaqīqah*, esoteric Knowledge, may appear as feminine.[16]

The Prophet said of himself: "The Law *(Sharī'ah)* is what I say; the Path *(Ṭarīqah)* is what I do; and Knowledge *(Ḥaqīqah)* is what I am." Now this third element, this "being," evokes a mystery of femininity in the sense that "being" transcends "thinking," represented by masculinity inasmuch as it may be conceived as lunar; woman offers happiness, not by her philosophy, but by her being. The crescent moon is so to speak "athirst" for plenitude, which is conceived as solar; thus the feminization of spiritual plenitude is partly explained by the fact that metaphysics is quite naturally in the hands of men.[17] But there is more: the feminine character that one can discern in Wisdom results moreover from the fact that the concrete knowledge of God

16. Echoes of this perspective are to be found in the Bible, notably in the Book of Wisdom and in Ecclesiasticus; thus under the sign of Solomon — which is not devoid of meaning, at least from the standpoint of the Kabalists.

17. In German, the word "sun" — *die Sonne* — is feminine, and the word "moon" — *der Mond* — is masculine; which evokes the perspective of matriarchy, of feminine priesthood, of women-prophetesses and obviously of shaktism. Tacitus made much of the great respect the Germans had for women. And let us recall here the beatific function of the Valkyries, and also this quasi-tantric sentence from Goethe: "The Eternal-Feminine draws us upwards" *(Das Ewig-Weibliche zieht uns hinan)*.

coincides with the love of God; this love, which to the extent it is sincere implies the virtues, is like the criterion of real knowledge. And it is in this sense that the saving *Shakti* is identified at once with Love and with Gnosis, with *Maḥabbah* and with *Ḥaqīqah*.

In his *Fuṣūṣ al-Ḥikam* — in the chapter on Muhammad — Ibn 'Arabi develops a doctrine which on the whole is shaktic and tantric, by taking as his point of departure the famous *ḥadīth* on women, perfumes and prayer: the "three things" that God "made lovable" to the Prophet. This symbolism signifies above all that for the male, woman occupies the center[18] among the objects of love, whereas all the other things that are naturally lovable — such as a garden, a piece of music, a glass of wine — are situated on the periphery, which is what the "perfumes" indicate; prayer represents the quintessential element — the relationship with the Sovereign Good — which gives meaning to everything else. Now according to Ibn 'Arabi, man, the male, loves woman as God loves man, the human being; for the whole loves its part, and the prototype loves its image; and this implies metaphysically and mystically the inverse movement, proceeding from the creature to the Creator and from woman to man. To say love, is to say desire for union, and

18. In Sufi mysticism the Divine Presence, or God Himself as object of love or of nostalgia, is readily presented as a woman. Let us quote the *Dīwān* of the Shaykh Al-'Alawi: "I drew near to Layla's dwelling, when I heard her call. O would that sweet voice never fall silent! She (Layla) favored me, drew me towards her, and took me into her precinct; then with words most intimate addressed me. She sat me by her, then came closer, and raised the garment that veiled her from my gaze; she took me out of myself, amazed me with her beauty . . . She changed me and transfigured me, marked me with her special seal, pressed me to her, granted me a unique station and named me with her name." The "divine dimension" is called Layla, "Night," for its a priori non-manifested quality; this makes one think of the dark color of Parvati and of the black Virgins in Christian art, and also, in a certain sense, of the nocturnal encounter between Christ and Nicodemus.

union is a relationship of reciprocity, whether it be between the sexes or between man and God.

In loving woman, man tends unconsciously towards the Infinite, and for that very reason he has to learn to do so consciously, by interiorizing and sublimizing the immediate object of his love; just as woman, in loving man, tends in reality towards the Absolute, with the same transpersonal virtualities.

*

* *

In the spiritually far-off world of the American Indians — which is basically a prolongation of Mongolian Shamanism — a typical personification of the *Shakti* is the "White Buffalo Cow Woman" who brought the Calumet to the tribe of the Lakota Indians.[19] In her celestial substance, she is the goddess Wohpé, who is the equivalent of Lakshmi; in her earthly apparition she is called Pté-San-Win, the "White Buffalo Cow Woman," precisely. A few centuries ago perhaps — no one knows the time or place — she appeared on earth dressed in white or red or, according to another tradition, completely naked; the color white, like nudity, refers to primordiality, and the color red refers to life, success, happiness. And it is always the goddess Wohpé who brings the smoke of the Calumet to Heaven, in that cloud containing man's offerings and prayers; offerings, because sacred tobacco is made of various ingredients symbolizing the elements of the universe, for the prayer of an individual must be implicitly that of the collectivity and even that of the entire world.

The rite of the Calumet evokes the symbolism of the sacrificial smoke, that which rises from altars: all ritual smoke is a support of the ascending grace offered by the

19. One no doubt meets with analogous, if not the same, accounts in other Indian tribes. In any case, the general symbolism has precedence over the particular "myth."

merciful *Shakti;* the same is true of the incense that carries our praises towards Heaven. For the American Indians, incense — the "sweet grass" of the prairie or some other aromatic plant — has a purifying function: every sacred object is purified before being used, including the human body prior to a rite such as the Sundance. Smoke is the sacramental matter used by the celestial Mediatrix; incense is like a veil that both envelops and manifests the invisible body of the goddess.

Smoke is an image of the breath; if the ritual smoke is sacred, so a fortiori is our breath whenever it is the vehicle of the Remembrance of God. And there is also a relationship between smoke and perfume; in the case of incense — including that of the Indians — both symbolisms are combined. Perfume expresses what in Arabic is termed *barakah,* which is not other than celestial or spiritual perfume; it emanates not only from saints and sacred things, but also from all that is agreeable to God, such as good actions and virtuous attitudes.

Flowers are loved for their perfume as well as for their beauty; now both these qualities relate to femininity and thus to the *Shakti;* beauty gladdens the heart and appeases it, and perfume makes one breathe, it evokes the limitlessness and purity of air; the "dilation of the breast," as one would say in Sufi mysticism.

*

* *

For the Hindus, every virtuous or beautiful women is in her way a manifestation of the *Shakti;* and if it can be said that virtue is a moral beauty, it can also be said that beauty is a physical virtue. The merit of this virtue devolves upon its Creator and, by participation, to the creature as well if she is morally and spiritually up to this gift; this is to say that beauty and virtue on the one hand pertain a priori to God, and on the other hand, for that very reason, demand that their spiritual implications be brought out by the creature.

The quality of *Shakti* in woman presupposes the quality of *Deva* in man; man by his nature is creator and master, unless he is perverted, but even then he keeps the shadows of his natural qualifications. Moreover, it goes without saying that each sex participates — or can participate — in the opposite sex;[20] the human quality is one and has primacy over the sex, but without in the least abolishing the latter's capacities, functions, duties and rights.

The character of *Deva* and *Shakti* show that the human being is, by definition, a theophany and that he has no choice but to be so, any more than he can choose not to be *homo sapiens.* The human vocation is to realize that which is man's reason for being: a projection of God and, therefore, a bridge between earth and Heaven; or a point of view that allows God to see Himself starting from an other-than-Himself, even though this other, in the final analysis, can only be Himself, for God is known only through God.

20. This is shown graphically by that fundamental symbol that is the Chinese *Yin-Yang,* which in all its applications expresses the principle of compensating reciprocity.

The Enigma of Diversified Subjectivity

To speak of a diversified, hence multiple, subjectivity, is no doubt inevitable since the world is what it is, yet it is nonetheless a contradiction in terms because, logically, subjectivity and plurality exclude each other. Indeed, the knowing subject is unique in the face of an indefinite multitude of objects known or to be known, and this irremovable — though illusory — uniqueness has about it something absolute from its own vantage point, that of consciousness precisely: no individual can cease being "I," and empirically there is no other "I" than his own.

The problem can be resolved only in a metaphysical reality, the invisible immanence of which eliminates the apparent absurdity of a subject that is on the one hand unique by definition and on the other as innumerable as the objects; the subject paradoxically becomes an object in its turn. For man, even the Divine Subject is an object, except at the summit of mystical union, that which gnosis[1] has in view.

We could also say that the disproportionate encounter between a contingent and possibly uninteresting subjectivity and the inexhaustible multitude of objects proves that at the

1. In India: *jnāna*, not *bhakti*. To say that God is "object" means, not that He is a "thing", but that He is the object of knowledge.

bottom of all subjectivity there is a subject proportioned to this dizzying multitude or to this grandeur: namely the absolute Subject, precisely. The prodigy does not lie in the myriad of objects which in principle may offer themselves to our perception, it is rather in subjectivity itself: "Heaven and earth cannot contain Me," says *Allāh* in a *ḥadīth,* "but the heart of the believer contains Me."

*

* *

Thus there is an absolute Subject that projects contingent subjects in a mysteriously contradictory, yet necessarily homogeneous, fashion. And this leads us to the crucial question of the worth of these subjects — if one may say so — hence also of their rights and duties. To say contingency is to say imperfection; the very contingency of multiplicable subjectivity excludes its perfection, and that is why the "human nature" of Christ could say: "Why callest thou me good? There is none good but one, that is, God." Contingency includes "mores" and "lesses," inequalities and fluctuations; it is impossible to introduce the absolute into contingency — without shattering it — unless it is a question of a "relative absoluteness," the possibility of which, precisely, proves that contingency could not be absolute and that it is of necessity belied, in its very substance, by the reflections of necessary Being.

The Islamic tradition also offers an example of the imperfection of contingency: the Prophet asked forgiveness of God every morning and evening, not because he had sinned, but because, in contingent existence, perfection is impossible; according to a *ḥadīth,* "Existence is a sin with which no other can be compared" — a daring expression to say the least, but heavy with meaning. Similarly, when a given Christian saint asserts that he is the greatest of sinners, one would like to paraphrase this expression by saying that he is the man most aware of the hazards of contingency; the idea that "the righteous man sins seven times daily,"[2] must be interpreted in this same sense.

Contingent and multiple subjectivity is imperfect, even "sinful," we have said. Now it is important to distinguish between a contingent subjectivity that is terrestrial and another that is celestial; the first one alone is imperfect and unstable, whereas the second, while being equally limited, is stable and exempt from sin by reason of the divine proximity offered by the ambience of Paradise. Terrestrial saints also are included to a certain degree in this rule, with the difference that they are not exempt from "slips," which the Moslem tradition attributes even to the Prophets, although they are judged impeccable.[3]

One can see from the preceding that it would be false to conclude that in contingency, hence in the world, "everything is relative," in the sense that there would be no clear-cut qualitative differences; once again we must have recourse to the notion of the "relatively absolute," for it goes without saying that Christ, while being in contingency and while asking "Why callest thou me good?" is good in a total and not merely partial or "relative" way. Besides, no virtuous man would say of himself that he is perfect, even though he might know that he is not bad — otherwise he would be devoid of intelligence — and that he might possibly have the right to defend himself against injustice, hence against error; for "there is no right superior to that of truth."[4] It is true that Christ attaches little worth to outward justification:

2. David even went so far as to say that "mine iniquities . . . are more than the hairs of mine head," which cannot be taken literally from an author of sacred texts.

3. The Koran (Sura "The Cave," 60-83) contains the story of the meeting between Moses and a mysterious personage who incarnates this "amoralism" that is metaphysically necessary by reason of the paradox included in All-Possibility.

4. Despite those curious "idealists" who think that evil lies in the ego and never elsewhere, whence a leveling that is always to the detriment of the good and to the advantage of the bad.

on the whole he asks us to renounce our "good right" and to care only for our innocence before God: now this is an ascetical and mystical standpoint that could take nothing away from the perspective of legitimate self-defense, so strongly affirmed in the Old Testament, hence by God Himself; every Christian will agree, and history proves it.

"The kingdom of God is within you," that is, in the spiritual, hence transpersonal, subjectivity; if such is the case, what can be the meaning of our outer life, of our contacts with beings and things? It is that positive phenomena manifest the heavenly treasures we bear within ourselves, and that they help us to uncover and realize them; we are fundamentally what we love,[5] and that is why we love it; the deepest subject rejoins the happiest shores. It is necessary to have the sense of beauty and the sense of the sacred, and also — on a much more modest plane — the sense of the divine perfume in the natural pleasures that life here below offers us, which implies that we partake of them with nobleness. "They have no wine," said the Holy Virgin at Cana; this saying can be understood at many levels, ranging from our right to earthly life to our duties in view of heavenly life.

*

* *

"God became man that man might become God": the absolute Subject, perfect in Itself, descended into contingency so that contingency could be reintegrated into the perfection of the absolute Subject. "I am the Way, the Truth, and the Life": Christ identifies himself with the divine Subjectivity, which "is incarnated" in the world of contingency, in conformity with the saving tendency of the Sovereign Good. The patristic saying just quoted also implies that such

5. Which makes us think of this saying of Saint Bernard: *O beata solitudo, o sola beatitudo* ("O beatific solitude, o sole beatitude"). It is a question of peace in God that nothing from without can replace; this peace which is the very substance of our deepest identity.

is the case with every human and prophetic theophany, whatever the mode of its manifestation. But above all and even a priori, this saying means that he who is "Way, Truth and Life" is the "I" as such, namely the Subject-Principle; this is to say that subjectivity, because it opens onto the Divine Self, comprises in its infinite substance an illuminating and liberating function. If "no man cometh unto the Father, but by me," it is because this "me" as such possesses a saving and unitive virtuality; every subjectivity as such is in principle a door towards its own transpersonal Essence.[6] God is intrinsically "I"; He is "He" only extrinsically and from man's vantage point, unless this personal pronoun is used independently of the opposition "subject-object," to designate the "suchness" of the Divine Reality; language in objective terms serves not only to indicate the complementary opposition in relation to the subject pole, but also — and much more generally — simply to express that which is. Besides, pure Being and absolute Consciousness coincide: "I am that I am"; Being and Consciousness also coincide with perfect Beatitude: *Sat, Chit, Ānanda;* "Being, Consciousness, Bliss."

God is the only and perfect Subject and His intent is to reintegrate the multiple and imperfect subjects; now in the divine intention, this paradoxical multiplicity also comprises — independently of its aspect of imperfection — a positive meaning, namely precisely the diversifying and boundless irradiation of All-Possibility; an irradiation that is produced in virtue of the "desire" of the Divine Self to manifest Itself in order that — in Islamic terms — the "hidden Treasure" might be known from without, starting from contingency,

6. It is in this sense that a Ramana Maharshi could reduce the whole problem of spirituality to the single question: "Who am I?" Which does not mean — as some imagine — that this question can constitute a path; on the one hand, it indicates the incommunicable state of the Maharshi, and on the other the principle of spiritual subjectivity, of the progressive participation in the pure Subject at once immanent and transcendant.

multiplicity, relativity; or again, so that God might be known "in" and "by" the world as well as "starting from" the world. *Ad majorem Dei gloriam;* the divine fan unfolds in joy and refolds in peace.

And this allows us to parenthetically state the following: Platonism, which is as it were "centripetal" and unitive, opens onto the consciousness of the one and immanent Self; on the contrary, Aristotelianism, which is "centrifugal" and separative, tends to sever the world — and with it man — from its divine roots. This can serve theology inasmuch as it needs the image of a man totally helpless without dogmatic and sacramental graces; and this led St. Thomas to opt for Aristotle — as against the Platonism of St. Augustine — and to deprive Catholicism of its deepest metaphysical dimension, while at the same time immunizing it — according to the usual opinion — against all temptation to "gnosis." Be that as it may, we could also say, very schematically, that Plato represents the inward dimension, subjective extension, synthesis and reintegration, whereas Aristotle represents the outward dimension, objective extension, analysis and projection; but this does not mean that Aristotle was a rationalist in the modern sense of the word. For the ancients, in fact, "reason" is synonymous with "intellect": reasoning prolongs intellection more or less, depending upon the level of the subject matter under consideration.

*

* *

The diversification of subjectivity has as an obvious consequence that, being a "particular subject" and not the "Subject as such," we are necessarily situated in a particular ambience and undergo by force of circumstances a particular destiny; this is to say that we pertain to the particular and not to the Universal; to possible being and not to necessary Being; to the relative good and not to the Sovereign Good. Living as we do in space and time, we are obliged — aside from our station before God — to be somewhere at a given moment and to undergo a given experience; and there is no need to be concerned because we are some particular person rather than some other. What counts is to maintain and strengthen our contact with the Universal, it being the essence of our particularity and thus of our relative qualities.

Space, time, object, subject: to remember God is to take refuge at the Center, in the Present, in pure Being, in the immanent Self, and thereby in immutable Beatitude.

Traces of Being, Proofs of God

According to the theologies, created things furnish a proof of God: starting from creatures, one infers the existence of a Creator. On this point, as on others, the theologians readily admit that reason can support dogma, and one need not blame them on this account for the generalized intellectual atrophy that justifies splitting the mind into two realms, belief and reasoning.[1]

For the metaphysician properly so called, who can be defined as having on the whole retained a primordial intelligence — and it is not disobliging to anyone to maintain that such men can still be found — for this metaphysician then, when faced with the divine mystery, it is not a matter of drawing "conclusions" from given "proofs," but on the contrary, of "perceiving" the transcendent Real through its "signs" or "traces"; it is to see the Cause in the effects, the Principle in its manifestations, the Archetypes or the Ideas in their projections, the Necessary in the possible.

1. It is to this infirmity become "natural" that these words of Christ refer a priori: "Blessed are they that have not seen, and yet have believed." A posteriori, it refers to the integration of the will into knowledge: "to see" is to know directly, and "to believe" is to behave as if one had this knowledge already; it is consequentiality and perfect sincerity. The unicity of the divine Object demands the totality of the human subject; this totality is "faith."

Phenomena "prove," or rather "manifest" divine Reality through several aspects: firstly through their existence pure and simple, secondly through the existential categories, such as space and time, and thirdly through qualities, which differentiate and arrange hierarchically such things as the elements, substances, forms; next, in the fourth place, come the faculties: vital, sensorial, mental, moral and intellectual or spiritual. Fifthly we could even mention privative phenomena, in the sense that the absence of a good proves, or indicates, the possibility of the presence of that good, *a contrario* and *ad majorem Dei gloriam;* an absence that cannot but be relative, since absolute evil does not exist.

But there are not only objective phenomena, there is also, and in a certain sense above all, the perceiving subjectivity, it too a "proof of God." The plurality of the conscious and knowing subject proves, by its very contradiction, the real unicity of an absolute underlying Subject; since logically there can be but a single subject — the consciousness of "I" being empirically unique — it is in the final analysis only the one Subject that is conceivable without absurdity, whatever be the mystery of its projections. In a word, the plurality of perceiving subjects can be explained only by the unicity of a unique immanent Subject.[2]

But let us return to the objective "signs" of God: the boundlessness of space, time, number, of formal differentiation, in short of the cosmic illimitation, indicates, by its very inconceivability — we would even say its absurdity — a transcendent dimension wherein the contradiction can and must be resolved; the empirical and extrinsic limitlessness must in a certain sense open onto a principial and intrinsic

2. The materialists, or some of them, would have us believe that the brain produces thoughts as an organ secretes fluids; this is to overlook what constitutes the very essence of thought, namely the materially unexplainable miracle of subjectivity: as if the cause of consciousness — immaterial and non-spatial by definition — could be a material object.

limitlessness, which is none other than the metaphysical or metacosmic Infinite. Analogous to what holds true for subjectivity, the boundlessness of the spatial and temporal conditions can only be explained by the immanence of a Principle-Infinitude, of which these conditions are the contingent projections, apparently contradictory since they depict the Infinite by the finite.

Be that as it may, we could imagine space as a spherical container; if one could traverse it, one would go in a circle, returning, doubtless not to the starting-point, but to a location as it were parallel to it, as regards the imaginary trajectory; this at least is one way of expressing the necessary limitation of manifested Illimitation.[3] Besides, it is appropriate not to forget that space coincides in fact with the ether, and time, with energy, the limits of which are perfectly conceivable; the possibility or impossibility of experiencing these limits is an altogether different question. In the same order of ideas, we would say that there is something mysterious and sacred in the point, the moment, unity, the sphere: they are so many openings towards divine prototypes, namely the Center, the Present, the One, the Perfect; whence their so to speak sacramental import. The divine signs — the "proofs of God" — are in the very structure of the world and of things.

Thus, our spirit perceives intellectually, and therefore intuitively, the Infinite in space and time, the Absolute or necessary Being in the existence of things, Perfection or the Good in qualities and faculties, and the supreme Self in the

3. Someone has said that "two parallel lines never meet, except in infinity, and since the latter does not exist, they remain separate"; this is a very curious combination of the obvious and the absurd. We would say that the reason for being of parallelism is separativity, and therefore that the lines need not meet any more than a circle is supposed to have angles; if both lines meet in infinity, it is not so that they might fuse, but so that they might rejoin their archetype, that of ontological parallelism: *Purusha* and *Prakriti,* the creative Essence that contains the potentialities, and the universal Substance that projects them into Existence.

prodigy of the perceiving subjectivity;[4] moreover — the importance of this argument authorizes us to repeat it — the phenomenon of an "I" that is unique, yet multiple in fact, is so contradictory — why is it that "I" am "I," why is the "other" an other?[5] — that, for whoever is sensitive to the essence of things, it necessarily opens onto the dazzling intuition of the absolute Subject, whose unicity, at once transcendent and immanent, is unambiguous.

*

*   *

Strictly speaking, the world is a fabric of theophanies; it could be nothing else, on pain of inexistence, for to exist is to express Being, in itself or in its potentialities. These theophanies — these divine traces — are more or less indirect, since they are not supernatural; it could be objected that in this case the term "theophany" is an abuse, but we employ it in order to indicate the deepest nature of existence and its modalities.[6] Thus, all natural theophanies are indirect, but this reservation does not preclude their being so to a greater or lesser degree as is proven, for example, by the distinction between the sacred and the profane in the human order. Outside this order, this distinc-

4. The Cartesian *cogito ergo sum* stops halfway; it would be necessary to add: "I am, therefore I am That which is," or even: "Being is, therefore I am"; the word "therefore" indicating here, not a conclusion, but a relationship of intellectually "visible" causality.

5. A contradiction that led Schopenhauer to think that solipsism cannot be refuted, but that solipsists ought to be put in an asylum. Solipsism is the demented antipode of the Vedantic doctrine of the Self; it shows in any case that there is an existentially paradoxical element in the empirical consciousness of the ego, which, far from granting the right to a senseless conclusion, in reality opens the way to the liberating truth. *Credo quia absurdum.*

6. In an analogous fashion, the expression "relatively absolute," which we sometimes employ, is paradoxical while being metaphysically useful or even necessary.

tion subsists in appropriate modes, which is to say that in nature there are phenomena that pertain analogically to the sacred and others that remain foreign to this excellence, as there are things or creatures that are noble and others that are not; but even the latter — as we have suggested above — have a theophanic character with respect to the prodigy of existence or with respect to some general qualities. Thus, very contemplative peoples, such as the Hindus and certain American Indians, have a tendency to universal adoration: to render homage to the divine traces even in modest things; this being an aspect of that pneumatic and primordial virtue that is the sense of the sacred.

When perceiving a sign-proof of the divine Principle, the contemplative mentality has two spontaneous reactions, namely essentialization and interiorization, the first being objective, and the second subjective: through the first, man sees in the sign or quality that which is essential — the divine intention if one will — whereas through the second, he finds the sign or quality in his own soul; on the one hand "unto the pure all things are pure"[7]; on the other, "the kingdom of God is within you." The first reaction refers to transcendence, and the second to immanence, although transcendence too relates to what we bear within ourselves, and although immanence also exists outside ourselves.

Thus, we live in a fabric of theophanies of which we are a part; to exist is to be a symbol; wisdom is to perceive the symbolism of things. And perhaps we ought to recall here the distinction between a symbolism that is direct, concrete, and evident, and another that — while being traditional — is indirect and more or less arbitrary with respect to formal

7. This formula first of all means that the Christian, inasmuch as he is an interiorized man who is outside the formalism of the Law, is supposed to have in view the nature of things and not human conventions; but it can also mean that the spiritual man everywhere sees substances and not accidents, the primordial divine intentions and not the earthly imperfections.

adequacy, which precisely it does not have in view. Direct symbolism "manifests" the reality symbolized, whereas indirect symbolism merely "indicates" a fragmentary, contingent or accidental aspect of the image chosen.[8] From another vantage point, we would say that the worship of symbols must obey sacramental rules: to worship the sun in place of God is one thing; to be aware of its spiritual emanation, and to know how to impregnate oneself with it ritually, is another.

*

* *

The contemplativity that allows of perceiving a trace of God in something created presupposes essentially the sense of forms and properties, which means that man ought to be able to see spontaneously, not only that something is beautiful and meaningful, but also why it is so; and this "why" coincides with the concrete vision of the celestial archetype or the divine aspect. In an altogether general way, a fundamental sensible phenomenon — the five elements offer examples of this — is not only a symbol, but also and thereby a trace of what it symbolizes; water is not merely an image of universal Substance, it is above all that Substance itself inasmuch as it appears on the material plane, or inasmuch as it is perceived by the gaze of relativity. Upon this vision of fundamental qualities or functions is superimposed the vision of multiple, more particular aspects, in short that of

8. Once again, it is necessary that the image be in conformity with the principles of sacred art; Plotinus said that the gods render themselves present in images that resemble them. Let it be noted that the idols of the Arabs were sites of magical powers; with the Jews, the golden calf and other idols materialized the nostalgia for a terrestrial god. Let us note at this point that, obviously, there are also negative symbols — that is, expressing privative realities — but it is of positive symbols and not of symbolism as such that we speak here.

the innumerable beauties or powers of the celestial Realm and of the Divine Nature.

What is true for the phenomena of the world is also true for those of the soul; the virtues are the traces of Heaven, or theophanies, just as are the beauties of nature or art; every fundamental virtue is a way of "seeing God" and ipso facto comprises a proof, or a sign, of the Sovereign Good. Moreover, to live a virtue, is not to appropriate it for oneself, it is to be penetrated by it; it does not mean to become puffed-up, but on the contrary to be extinguished, and in becoming extinguished to find a new life which in reality is our essence and our primordial nature.

Saving Dimensions

The destiny of creatures is determined either by an inexorable causality, or by the free intervention of a saving grace; the law of *karma* and the mystery of *kripā*. Both dimensions are rooted in the same Divine Reality, namely, respectively, in its Absoluteness and in its Infinitude; we could also say: in Being and in Possibility.

It is in this ambiguity that resides the entire apparent paradox of predestination combined with freedom. The Hindus readily argue, against the Semitic dogma of predestination, that the theory of good and bad *karma* — the law of actions and concordant reactions — is more satisfying, logically and morally, than the Semitic idea of fatality. However, this polemic argument merely pushes back the limits of the difficulty, since it does not explain the origin of the chain of causes and effects. In a total individual cycle, there must evidently be an initial action that provokes an initial cosmic or divine reaction, and it remains an open question as to what cause determined this initial action — meritorious or culpable — of the creature; for, starting from the premises of the Hindu doctrine, one is indeed obliged to agree that "transmigration" has a beginning. Independently of this doctrine, Ibn 'Arabi properly teaches that it is not God who creates responsible creatures ab extra, but that on the contrary the creatures are a priori that which they "want to be" in the order of All-Possibility, and that God merely transfers them from this order into existence; the individual "creates himself" in the principial order, and his subsequent actions are merely the manifestations of the particular possibility he represents; a possibility is simply what it is or what it must be, and not what someone else wants it to be.

The existence of the responsible individuality being granted — whatever might be its explanation — we must distinguish in God a dimension of Justice and another of Mercy; and we must in addition distinguish between paths of salvation relating to one or the other of these two aspects, or perhaps to their combination. This is the as it were classical opposition between a path of action and merit, and a path of grace; but in fact, whatever the accent given to either of these perspectives, the man mindful of his salvation cannot help putting into motion all that he is, hence to act, to love and to think; which corresponds respectively to the three fundamental paths of *karma, bhakti* and *jnāna.*

*

* *

As the very notion of *jnāna* indicates, there are not only the dimensions of Justice and Mercy, there is also in the divine Nature, and thus in spirituality, a third saving dimension, which is Gnosis both divine and human, a priori discriminative and a posteriori unitive; this dimension is based on the spiritual homogeneity of the Universe. Gnosis frees in virtue of the profound and, as it were, immanent identity between the human "I," *jīvātmā,* and the divine "Self," *Ātmā;* something which neither the partisans of meritorious action nor those of redemptive faith are ready to acknowledge, since they see in Gnosis a solution of easiness and a usurpation of what they consider to be their exclusive spiritual rights. In reality, the *jnānī* — the man of Gnosis — integrates both action and faith or love in his path; not because he believes that these positions free him by themselves, but because they act as supports — or because they are concomitants — of his liberating knowledge, or let us say of his intuition of universal Unity. For on the one hand, like it or not, the rightly intentioned utterance of a sacred formula — and man is essentially a speaking being — is a meritorious action; and on the other hand, there is no intellective awareness that goes without an element of faith, of *shraddhā,* hence of grace and trust. In a word, one does not "realize" the Impersonal without the help of the Personal God.

The partisans of meritorious action readily argue that only action, being an objective factor, comprises a predictable certitude, whereas faith and knowledge, being subjective factors, remain uncertain and precarious; obviously, they do not perceive the elements of objectivity comprised in ways other than theirs. The partisans of faith for their part argue that only faith issuing from the awareness of our powerlessness has the capacity to move the Divinity; Mercy irresistibly saves those who open themselves to it; our actions and our knowledge cannot add anything. From the standpoint of unitive and liberating knowledge, on the contrary, no legitimate perspective is condemned; the efficacy of the two other standpoints mentioned is acknowledged, but with the reservation that *jnāna* alone enables one to attain the supreme goal, or to attain it in a direct manner. In other words, for *jnāna,* the two other ways — *karma-mārga* and *bhakti*— are steps toward the summit of celestial possibilities, the *Brahma-Loka.*[1]

*
* *

According to a Hindu formula, "the majesty of the Law is wedded to the forgiving compassion of Love"; this is what the divine couples express, the masculine pole manifesting Rigor, hence Justice, and the feminine pole Gentleness,

1. Which is *Sat, Chit* and *Ānanda:* Being, Consciousness and Beatitude.

hence Mercy. These two poles — or these two dimensions — of the Divinity seem to contradict each other, not with respect to their complementarity of course, but with respect to their opposition; inexorable Justice seems to be incompatible with freely given Mercy. Now both principles are rooted in a higher "divine logic" which resolves their opposition: this is All-Possibility, woven of absoluteness and infinitude.

The whole mystery of these two dimensions at first glance irreconcilable — Justice and Mercy — finally resides in the difference of the possible relationships between *Ātmā* and *Māyā,* the Absolute and the Relative; one relationship being separative, discontinuous and based on transcendence, and the other being unitive, continuous and based on immanence. This is, geometrically speaking, the difference between a system of concentric circles and a system of centrifugal or centripetal radii.

We could also say that Relativity, *Māyā,* implies on the one hand a radiation, and on the other hand an unfolding; the first function corresponds to the centrifugal radii, and the second to the concentric circles. Now the cosmogonic and creative radiation, as we have often remarked, implies by definition an increasing distance with respect to the Divine Source, whereas the unfolding in *Māyā* of possibilities contained in *Ātmā* implies oppositions; whence the phenomenon of evil, and whence too the principle of Justice; but the very homogeneity of the Universe — being of divine essence — implies in its turn the principle of Mercy. And one must not lose sight of the following: on the plane of radiation, there is not merely increasing remoteness, there is also drawing closer; and on the plane of unfolding or of diversity, there are not merely oppositions, there are also complementarities.

It is thus that in the economy of *Ātmā-Māyā* a negative element is always compensated by a positive element; this is necessarily the case because "*Māyā* is *Ātmā,*" which is to say that Relativity is nothing other than a play of mirrors by which *Ātmā,* as *Ānanda,* enjoys its own potentialities.

Part Two

Fundamental Perspectives

Man in the Face of the Sovereign Good

Man is first of all characterized by a central or total intelligence, and not one that is merely peripheral or partial; secondly he is characterized by a free and not merely instinctive will; and thirdly by a character capable of compassion and generosity, and not merely of egoistic reflexes.

As for animals, they cannot know what is beyond the senses, even though they may be sensitive to the sacred; they cannot choose against their instincts, even though they may instinctively make a sacrifice; they cannot transcend themselves, even though an animal species may manifest nobility.

Of man it may also be said that he is essentially capable of knowing the True, whether it be absolute or relative; he is capable of willing the Good, whether it be essential or secondary, and of loving the Beautiful, whether it be interior or exterior. In other words: the human being is substantially capable of knowing, willing and loving the Sovereign Good.

The Sovereign Good, we have said, and this is to say the Supreme Principle. When we speak of the "Supreme Principle," our only terrestrial point of reference is the existence of things; whereas when we speak of the "Sovereign Good," we may refer to their qualities, which are morally as well as aesthetically tangible to us. To speak of the "Sovereign Good," is to attest that all goods derive from It and bear witness to It, and it is to open the door to the "remembrance" of the normative and at the same time liberating archetypes.

Starting from the idea that man is total intelligence, free will and generous soul, we arrive at this ternary: Truth, Way and Virtue; in other words: metaphysical and cosmological doctrine, spiritual method and moral quality. "Wisdom, Strength, Beauty."

*

* *

Transcendence, immanence and theophany: these are the three relationships through which man can approach Divine Reality. This means that it is in man's nature to be able to approach God, firstly in a direct and objective manner, secondly in an indirect but also objective manner, and thirdly in a manner that is direct and subjective: thus firstly by addressing himself to the personal God, who is outside and above us, then by addressing himself to a given human manifestation of God, and finally by finding God in the depths of his heart. This is first the transcendent God enthroned in Heaven, then the Man-God or, more generally, the Symbol and the Sacrament; and finally the immanent Self.

Metaphysically, it is important to distinguish between a transcendence that is objective and another that is paradoxically subjective; analogously, within immanence a subjective aspect must be distinguished from an objective aspect; similarly again, there is not only a manifested theophany, but also a principial one.

In itself, transcendence is objective by definition; if it can comprise an aspect of subjectivity it is because the immanent Self remains transcendent with respect to the "I," which nonetheless prolongs the Self in a certain fashion. As for immanence, it is subjective a priori, at least from the standpoint taken here; it is nonetheless objective in the phenomena surrounding us, which would have neither existence nor power without an immanent divine presence.

And by definition, theophany is manifested: however, this manifestation itself implies — and proves — that it is necessarily prefigured in the divine Order by the personal God who is none other — if one may so put it — than the hypostatic "manifestation" of the impersonal or, more precisely, suprapersonal Divinity.

*

* *

The following must be insisted upon: it is in the nature of things that man have two connections with God, one direct and another indirect; this results from his very existence, which is to say that it results from the duality "Principle and Manifestation"; *Ātmā* and *Māyā.* On the one hand man is alone before God; on the other hand, he addresses himself to an intermediary celestial interlocutor: the Logos, which by definition combines the Divine and the human; in both cases, it is de facto God who listens and replies. We have said that this is in the nature of things: even Islam, so jealously unitarian, cannot help attributing to its Prophet the function of intercessor; and Buddhism, implacable negator of the gods, is obliged to recognize the reality of an *Amitābha* or an *Avalokiteshvara* mercifully holding out a hand to powerless man.

In fact, none of the three perspectives can suffice unto itself, advaitic immanentism no more than religious transcendentisms and theosophisms: Shankaracharya wrote hymns to the Goddess. There is no subjective realization possible without the benediction of an objective Divinity, despite pseudo-jnanic simplifiers who teach the contrary.

In Itself, the Supreme Principle is neither transcendent nor immanent, It "is That which is"; only in relation to Manifestation may one speak either of transcendence or of immanence. And transcendence and immanence are united in theophany: in the Logos, the Man-God, the *Avatāra,* and in a certain manner also in the Divine Symbol and the saving Sacrament.

In the final analysis, there is only one distinction to be made, that of transcendence and immanence; theophany is simply a mode of the second mystery. One may therefore say transcendence annihilates, reduces or diminishes the manifested; immanence on the contrary ennobles, dilates or magnifies it. On the one hand, man is "sinner" or "slave" — according to religious language — but on the other hand, he is "child of God" or "vicar on Earth." Both relationships come together in a particularly expressive way in the Man-God: on the one hand, "God alone is good"; but on the other: "He that hath seen me hath seen the Father."

*

* *

Unquestionably, Judaism and Islam accentuate transcendence, whereas Christianity is founded upon theophany; Buddhism takes its point of departure in the mystery of immanence. Each of these standpoints negates or limits a priori the others, but realizes them a posteriori in a way suitable to its perspective. Compared to Judaism, Christianity moreover comprises a certain accentuation of the element of immanence, whence its near rejection of outer prescriptions and its insistence upon inner qualities. And Buddhism necessarily combines its initial immanentism — its cult of *Nirvāna,* "inward" by definition — with a theophanism that is both exclusive and inclusive: in principle there is only a single Buddha, but his mystery is nonetheless manifested in a profusion of divine personifications.[1]

*

* *

The situation of man in the face of God evokes the question of knowing which hypostatic mode or ontological

1. Cf. our article "Orthodoxy and Originality of Buddhism" in *In the Tracks of Buddhism,* (Unwin-Hyman, London, 1989).

degree is involved in this confrontation. We would reply a priori with the following images: first of all there is limitless space; then there is the sun; and finally there is the reflection — or reflections — of the sun. These images may symbolize, respectively, Beyond-Being, Being and Existence; the last term meaning here the divine Center of the Universe, namely the manifested divine Principle, or in other words, the cosmic projection of God.

This is the metaphysical — not theological — Trinity, which may be qualified as "vertical." But there is also a "horizontal" Trinity, situated, with the appropriate differences, on each of the levels just mentioned. Thus on the level of Being — which is that of the personal God, hence also that of theology — we shall discern the Essence, then the "Form" or the "Image," and then Radiation. This Trinity is necessarily anticipated in Beyond-Being, which comprises the aspects of Absoluteness, Infinity and All-Possibility. Below Being, hence on the level of Existence or more exactly at its Divine Center, which is the direct reflection of the Principle in Manifestation, the "horizontal" Trinity will comprise firstly the always principial or divine Essence, then the Personification — or archangelic personifications — of this Essence, and finally the Radiation of the Logos in the world and in souls.

Man's only possible relationship with Beyond-Being is in pure Intellection and, in principle — *Deo volente* — in contemplative concentration. The relationship with Being — and it is this alone that religions have in view — is realized through prayer, the virtues, comportment; the same relationship will be realized indirectly through an *Avatāra*, or quite generally, through a Symbol.

*
* *

Beyond-Being, Being and Existence: each of these levels of the "vertical" Trinity can be viewed either with respect to transcendence or to immanence or again to theophany.

There is no difficulty in conceiving the transcendence and immanence of Beyond-Being and Being, but it may be asked what these two aspects mean on the level of theophanic projection; the answer is that the Logos — the *Avatāra* — presents himself either objectively as "Divine Image," in which case he is transcendent in relation to ordinary men, or subjectively as the Intellect, in which case he is immanent; he is then like the door towards the Divine Self, the immanent Divine Subject in our immortal substance.[2]

As for the presence of the element "theophany" in Being and Beyond-Being, it is there as pure potentiality: it is above all the intrinsic possibility of Radiation proper to the Divine Essence and thus to each of its ontological levels, as we have explained above. One will have seen that the element "Existence" in the vertical Trinity coincides in a certain respect with the element "theophany," hence with the theophanic perspective added to the perspectives of transcendence and immanence. For Existence, whether celestial or terrestrial, central or peripheral, is not other than the universal theophany, connected to Being from the standpoint of transcendence, and to the Self from the standpoint of immanence.

The question of knowing to which "divine level" man must address himself when praying never ought to arise, for to pray is to speak to God, independently of any metaphysical specification; the man who prays, even if he addresses a celestial personification, should not concern himself with the ontology of the celestial Interlocutor. On the one hand, "the kingdom of God is within you"; and on the other hand,

2. Of course, our intention is not to reduce all the Real and all the Possible to the single metaphysical analysis presented here. Other analyses will be found in most of our books; by way of providing a starting point, we may refer the reader to *Survey of Metaphysics and Esoterism* (World Wisdom Books, Bloomington, Indiana, 1986). We have said "analyses"; we could also have said "syntheses."

"he that hath seen me hath seen the Father." But also, and above all: "Our Father who art in Heaven."

Outline of the Christian Message

If we start from the incontestable idea that the essence of all religions is the truth of the Absolute with its human consequences, mystical as well as social, the question may be asked how the Christian religion satisfies this definition; for its central content seems to be not God as such but Christ; that is, not so much the nature of the Divine Being as its human manifestation. Thus a Patristic voice proclaimed pertinently: "God became man that man might become God"; this is the Christian way of saying that "Brahman is real, the world is appearance." Christianity, instead of simply juxtaposing the Absolute and the contingent, the Real and the illusory, proposes initially the reciprocity between the one and the other: it sees the Absolute a priori in relation to man, and man — correlatively — is defined in conformity with this reciprocity, which is not only metaphysical, but also dynamic, voluntary, eschatological. It is true that Judaism proceeds in an analogous fashion, but to a lesser degree: it does not define God in relation to the human drama, hence starting from contingency, but it does establish the quasi-absolute relationship between God and His people; God is "the God of Israel," the symbiosis is immutable; however God remains God, and man remains man; there is no "human God" or "divine man."

Be that as it may, the reciprocity posed by Christianity is metaphysically transparent, and it is necessarily so, on pain of being an error. Unquestionably, once we are aware of the

Reality: in Christianity, as in every other religion, there are fundamentally two things to consider, abstractly and concretely: the Absolute, or the absolutely Real, which is the Sovereign Good and which gives meaning to everything; and our consciousness of the Absolute, which must become second nature for us, and which frees us from the meanderings, impasses and abysses of contingency. The rest is a matter of adaptation to the needs of given souls and societies; but the forms also have their intrinsic worth, for the Truth wills beauty, in its veilings as well as in ultimate Beatitude.

*
* *

Intrinsically Christian, non-Hellenized, metaphysics is expressed by the initial sayings of the Gospel of St. John. "In the beginning was the Word": obviously, what is meant is not a temporal origin but a principial priority, that of the divine Order, to which the universal Intellect — the Word — pertains, while nonetheless being linked to cosmic manifestation, of which It is the center both transcendent and immanent. "And the Word was with God": with respect to Manifestation precisely, the Logos is distinguished from the Principle, while being "with" It through its essence. "And the Word was God": with respect to the Divine Order, the Logos is not distinct from the Principle; the distinction between the two natures of Christ reflects the inevitable ambiguity of the realtionship *Ātmā-Māyā*. "All things were made by him": there is nothing created that was not conceived and prefigured in the divine Intellect. "And the light shineth in darkness; and the darkness comprehended it not": it is in the nature of *Ātmā* to penetrate into *Māyā*, and it is in the nature of a certain *Māyā* to resist it,[5] otherwise the

5. What is in question here is the negative dimension proper to subcelestial *Māyā*, which is made of darkness inasmuch as it becomes distant from the Principle, and of light inasmuch as it manifests aspects of the

world would cease to be the world; and "it must needs be that offences come." Christ's victory over the world and over death retraces or anticipates the victory — as such timeless — of Good over Evil, or of Ormuzd over Ahriman; a victory that is ontologically necessary because it results from the nature of Being itself, despite initial appearances to the contrary. The darkness, even in winning, loses; and the light, even in losing, wins; Passion, Resurrection, Redemption.

Principle. It is the domain of imperfection and impermanence, but also of potentially liberating theomorphism, whereas the heavenly *Māyā* is the domain of the archetypes and the Hypostases.

Outline of the Islamic Message

The enigma of the lightning-like expansion of Islam and its adamantine stability lies in the fact that it has given a religious form to that which constitutes the essence of all religion. And it is in this sense that some Sufis have said that, being the terminal religion, Islam is ipso facto the synthesis of the preceding religions — the synthesis and thereby the archetype. Terminality and primordiality rejoin.

On the surface of Islam we meet with the features of the Bedouin mentality, which obviously have nothing universal about them; in the fundamental elements, however, we encounter as it were religion as such, which by its essentiality opens quite naturally onto metaphysics and gnosis.

All metaphysics is in fact contained in the Testimony of Faith *(Shahādah)*, which is the pivot of Islam.[1] Exoterically, this Testimony means that only creative Being is the supreme Principle that determines everything; esoterically, it means in addition — or rather a priori — that only Beyond-Being is the intrinsic Absolute, since Being is the Absolute only in relation to Existence: this is the distinction between *Ātmā* and *Māyā*, which is the very substance of esoterism. "Neither I (the individual) nor Thou (the Divine Person), but He (the Essence)": it is starting from this Sufic saying that the pro-

1. "There is no divinity if not the (sole) Divinity *(Allāh)*." This may be compared with the Vedantic formulation: "*Brahman* is real, the world is an appearance."

noun "He" has often been interpreted as meaning the impersonal Essence; and the same meaning has been attributed to the final breath of the Name *Allāh.* After the Testimony of Faith, in the order of the "Pillars of the Religion" *(Arqān ad-Dīn),* comes Prayer *(Ṣalāt):* the human discourse addressed to the Divinity, which is of primary importance since we are beings endowed with intelligence,[2] hence with speech; not to speak to God, yet to speak to men, amounts to denying God and His Lordship. The intention of primordiality, in Islam, is manifested by the fact that every man is his own priest; primordial man — or man in conformity with his profound nature — is a priest by definition; without priesthood, there is no human dignity. The meaning of prayer is to become aware — always anew — of total Reality, then of our situation in the face of this reality; hence to affirm the necessary relationships between man and God. Prayer is necessary, not because we do or do not possess a given spiritual quality, but because we are men.

The Testimony and Prayer are unconditional; the Tithe *(Zakāt)* is conditional in the sense that it presupposes the presence of a human collectivity. On the one hand it is socially useful and even necessary; on the other hand it conveys the virtues of detachment and generosity, lacking which we are not "valid interlocutors" before God.

As for the Fast *(Ṣiyām)* — practiced during Ramadan — it is necessary because asceticism, like sacrifice in general, is a fundamental possibility of human behavior in the face of the cosmic *māyā;* every man must resign himself to it to one degree or another. In fact, every man, whether he likes it or not, experiences pleasure, and thus must also experience renunciation, as he opts for Heaven; to be man is to be capable of transcending oneself. However, Islam is well

2. We could say "endowed with reason," but it is not reason as such which counts, it is integral intelligence of which reason is only the discursive mode.

aware of the rights of nature: all that is natural and normal, and lived without avidity and without excess, is compatible with the spiritual life and can even assume in it a positive function.[3] Nobility is here the awareness of the archetypes, and above all the sense of the sacred; only he who knows how to renounce can enjoy nobly, and this is one of the meanings of the Fast.

*

* *

Unlike the Testimony of Faith, the Prayer, the Fast, and to a certain extent the Tithe, the Pilgrimage and the Holy War are conditional: the Pilgrimage depends on our capacity to accomplish it, and the Holy War is obligatory only under certain circumstances. We need not take into consideration here the fact that every obligation of the religion — except for the Testimony — is conditional in the sense that there may always be unavoidable obstacles; the Law never demands anything impossible or unreasonable.

The meaning of the Pilgrimage *(Ḥajj)* is the return to the origin, thus what is involved is a lived affirmation of primordiality; of recontacting the original Benediction, Abrahamic in the case of Islam. But there is also, according to the Sufis, the Pilgrimage towards the heart: towards the immanent sanctuary, the divine kernel of the immortal soul.

In an analogous fashion, there is, along with the outer Holy War *(Jihād)*, the "Greater Holy War" *(al-Jihād al- akbar)*, that which man wages against his fallen and concupiscent soul; its weapon is fundamentally the "Remembrance of God" *(Dhikru 'Llāh)*, but this combat presupposes nonetheless our moral effort. The all-embracing virtue of "poverty" *(faqr)* is conformity to the demands of the Divine Nature: namely effacement, patience, gratitude, generosity; and

3. This is what is expressed and in principle realized in every religion by the formulas of consecration such as the *benedicite* or the *basmalah.*

also, and even above all, resignation to the Will of God and trust in His Mercy. Clearly, the goal of the inner Holy War is perfect self-knowledge, beyond the veils of passion; for "whoso knoweth his soul, knoweth his Lord."

To return to the Testimony of Faith: to believe in God is to believe also in that which God has done and will do: it is to believe in the Creation, in the Prophets, in the Revelation, in the Afterlife, in the Angels, in the Last Judgement. And to believe is to acknowledge sincerely, drawing the consequences from what one believes; "belief obligates," we could say. Whence the crucial importance, in the thought and sensibility of Islam, of the virtue of sincerity *(ṣidq),* which coincides with "right doing" *(iḥsān),* whether it be a question of religious zeal or esoteric deepening.[4] Theologically, one distinguishes faith *(īmān),* practice *(islām)* and their quality *(iḥsān),* the "right doing," precisely; and this latter, according to a Muhammadan saying, consists in "worshipping God as if thou seest Him; and if thou dost not see Him, He nonetheless seeth thee."

4. Echoing the parable of the talents, St. James in his Epistle says that "to him that knoweth to do good, and doeth it not, to him it is sin;" which is to say that God requires wisdom of him who possesses it potentially; whence the inclusion of esoteric spirituality *(taṣawwuf)* in *iḥsān.*

Pillars of Wisdom

What a priori characterizes the difference between exoterism and esoterism, is that the starting point of the former is an anthropomorphic faith combined with a voluntaristic, individualistic and sentimental piety, whereas the starting point of the latter is an intellectual discernment combined with an accentuation of intrinsic and inward values. When speaking of discernment, we mean above all that between the Real and the illusory, *Ātmā* and *Māyā,* the Absolute and the relative, necessary Being and possible Being; a distinction that implies on the one hand the prefiguration of the relative in the Absolute, and on the other the projection of the Absolute into the relative, hence all the degrees and modes of universal Reality.[1] The "prefiguration" of the relative in the Absolute is the Creator-Being with all the potentialities contained therein; the "projection" of the Absolute into the relative is the "Spirit of God," the celestial world, the universal Intellect, the *Avatāra,* Revelation; but also, the theomorphic microcosm, the human Intellect, the "naturally supernatural" prodigy of intellection; the organ of the *Sophia Perennis,* precisely.

1. And let us recall that *Māyā* does not coincide purely and simply with the manifested Universe, since — beyond the Universe — it encompasses Being itself; that is to say that the discernment between "God" and the "world" is metaphysically less rigorous and less fundamental than that between *Ātmā* and *Māyā,* "Reality" and "illusion."

*
* *

Metaphysical discernment essentially comprises two exigencies, on pain of remaining spiritually inoperative: firstly, self-knowledge; and secondly, consciousness — in principle permanent — of absolute Reality. Self-knowledge is an exigency at once logical and moral: logical, because discernment of the Absolute includes discernment of the relative, and because discernment of the Transcendent entails that of the Immanent; and moral, because purely cerebral knowledge — not in itself, but by its fragmentariness which in fact is unrealistic — isolated from its necessary human context, greatly risks producing psychic disorders: namely temptations of self-sufficiency, narcissism and pride. And this has always furnished the spokesmen for exoterism with an easy argument against gnosis; quite mistakenly, of course, since authentic esoterism is initiatory by definition and could not stop at theory alone; to know is to be.

The moral exigency of metaphysical discernment means that virtue is part of wisdom; a wisdom without virtue is in fact imposture and hypocrisy, doubtless not initially, but certainly in the long run. We may also point out that plenary knowledge of Divine Reality presupposes or demands moral conformity to this Reality, as the eye necessarily conforms to light; since the object to be known is the Sovereign Good, the knowing subject must correspond to it analogically. Or again: the qualification for knowledge is essentially objectivity, not only in relation to universal principles, but also in relation to the knowing subject; and this second objectivity implies virtue, precisely. One cannot know the grandeur of the Absolute without knowing correlatively the smallness of the contingent, thus of man; to neglect this consciousness of human littleness, is to put in its place a false greatness; in a word, only he who is disposed to know himself is qualified for knowledge of the Transcendent. Virtue, which logically and practically results from self-knowledge, is all the more indispensable in spiritual alchemy since it opens onto the mystery of Immanence.

We have said that the second exigency of integral discernment is the permanent awareness of the Sovereign Good. If God is "all that is," knowledge of Him requires "all that we are"; now we are, among other things, our entire life, thus we must integrate our entire life into the knowledge of God. In duration, we never cease being ourselves, so that duration is an aspect of our being; and to be aware of the Real, is to be aware of it always. To fully discern metaphysical Truth — fully, that is to say in accordance with what is demanded by its very nature — is to assimilate, hence realize it; all the more so in that the Supreme Reality is, in the final analysis, our own reality. Realized knowledge — not merely thought — is to theory what the sphere is to the circle or the cube to the square, geometrically speaking; holiness is a dimension of wisdom; the Ancients were far from being unaware of this.

*

* *

The fact that the subject amounts to a dimension of the object, rather as time is in a sense a dimension of space — this fact shows how important the perspective of "inwardness" is in the face of God; that is, the accentuation of inward, intrinsic, profound qualities, and by way of consequence the concern to avoid the pitfall of superficial formalism. Christ intended that one adore God "in spirit and in truth," and not by "the prescriptions of men"; he opposed inward, and by definition sincere, values to outward and extrinsic attitudes; and this, if it is not esoterism pure and simple, is at least one of its fundamental dimensions. "The kingdom of God is within you"; this refers metaphysically to the divine "Self," to the immanent *Ātmā;* hence to the "uncreated and uncreatable" Intellect of the Eckhartian doctrine.

"The world is false, *Brahman* is true; the soul is not other than *Brahman.*" This Vedantic formula furnishes the key of the principle of inwardness: which means that we can attain the divine Self only within ourselves, given that it is our essence. Moreover, it is this mystery of potential or virtual identity that explains the secretiveness of esoterism.[2]

In a more elementary mode, inwardness is faith, which by its very nature frees from formalistic and legalistic servitude, and which essentially saves us; however, more profoundly, inwardness is union with the immanent divine Presence and, in the final analysis, with the divine Self. This dimension of depth does not, of course, abolish faith, but on the contrary includes and "essentializes" it; if faith can save us, that is because it is, at the level it pertains to, a mode of our paradisiacal essence. Intelligence is to discern transcendent Reality; inwardness is to unite oneself with immanent Reality; the one does not go without the other. Discernment, by its nature, calls forth union; both elements imply virtue by way of consequence and even a priori.

Discernment and union, we have said; analogously, we may distinguish between "comprehension" and "concentration," the latter referring to the "heart" or to "life," and the former to the "mind" or to "thought"; although there is also on the one hand a mental concentration, and on the other, and even before thought, a cardiac comprehension, namely intellection.

2. According to Plutarch, Alexander the Great received from Aristotle not only the doctrines concerning morality and politics, but also "those enigmatic and profound" theories that certain masters intended to "reserve for oral communication for initiates, without allowing many to learn about them." Having heard that Aristotle had published some of these teachings, Alexander reproached him in a letter; but Plutarch assures us that the books of Aristotle treating of metaphysics are "written in a style that renders them unusable for the ordinary reader, and useful only as memoranda for those who already have been instructed in this subject." Let us add however that according to the Kabbalists, "it is better to divulge wisdom than to forget it"; this is perhaps what Joachim of Fiore thought of when foreseeing an "age of the Spirit."

*

* *

The quality of inwardness demands of us not a renunciation of the outward world — which, besides, would be impossible — but an equilibrium determined by the spiritual meaning of the world and of life. The vice of outwardness is the lack of harmony between the two dimensions: between our tendency towards the things that surround us and our tendency towards the "kingdom of God which is within you." What is necessary is to realize a spiritual rootedness that removes from outwardness its tyranny at once dispersing and compressing, and that on the contrary allows us to "see God everywhere"; which means to perceive symbols, archetypes and essences in sensible things, for the beauties perceived by an interiorized soul become factors of interiorization. Similarly regarding matter: what is necessary is not to deny it — if that were possible — but to withdraw from its seductive and enslaving grasp; to distinguish in it what is archetypal and quasi-celestial from what is accidental and indeed too earthly; hence to treat it with nobleness and sobriety.

In other words, outwardness is a right, and inwardness a duty; we have the right to outwardness because we belong to this spatial, temporal and material world, and we must realize inwardness because our spiritual nature is not of this world, nor, consequently, is our destiny. God is generous: when we withdraw towards the inward, it will, in compensation, manifest itself for us in the outward; nobleness of soul is to have the sense of the divine intentions, hence of the archetypes and essences, which readily reveal themselves to the noble and contemplative soul. Conversely, when we withdraw towards the heart, we will find therein all the beauties perceived outwardly; not as forms, but in their quintessential possibilities. In turning towards God, man can never lose anything.

Thus, when man interiorizes himself, God so to speak exteriorizes Himself while enriching man from within; there lies all the mystery of the metaphysical transparency of phenomena and of their immanence in us. In exoterism, beauty is merely a "sensible consolation," and it is even considered a two-edged sword, an invitation to sin and a concession unworthy of a perfect ascetic, which implies that asceticism — the renunciation of the agreeable things earth can offer us — is the only way that leads to God.[3] In reality, and by the nature of things, nothing that nature offers us is in itself a spiritual obstacle; quite the contrary, the fact that nature grants us a given "consolation" — the very fact that it is nature granting it and that we invent nothing — this fact proves that the "consoling" gift possesses a sacramental virtuality, whether we are capable of grasping it or not. The first condition of this capacity is — we emphasize — elevation of character, hence also the sense of the sacred; for only beauty of soul allows of spiritually assimilating the beauty of things.[4]

It follows from all this that outwardly perceived beauty — the knight's "lady" for example or the work of sacred art — must be discovered or realized inwardly, for we love that which we are and we are that which we love. Perceived beauty is not only the messenger of a heavenly and divine archetype, it is also, and for that very reason, the outward projection of a universal quality immanent in us, and quite obviously more real than our empirical and imperfect ego gropingly seeking its identity.

*
* *

3. The cult of emptiness of certain Christian and Buddhist monks does not necessarily pertain to this manner of seeing things.

4. There is assuredly a false inwardness, and it is narcissism; but in this case, the inward is merely a relatively exterior layer of the personality, namely the empirical ego; access towards the true interior is blocked and there can be no question of moral beauty.

It is upon these truths — aside from other bases — that not only alchemical hermeticism and knightly initiation are founded, but also various artisanal initiations, which include the arts properly so called. This implies that a science and an activity can serve as a spiritual support to the extent that they are natural, useful and necessary to man. Since this possibility of a way founded upon a natural, and ipso facto symbolical, activity is inscribed in the very nature of the human being, it necessarily has to manifest itself, and this independently of the religious phenomenon and parallel to it; the question of knowing whether or not it does double duty along with religion can arise in theory, but it has no concrete bearing, since man is a complex being and since he will in any case make use of his various faculties.

Let us recall in this connection that the common religion is all that it has to be: its aim is to save as many souls as possible and therefore it offers what is at once "indispensable for every man and accessible to every intelligence," according to a Guénonian expression. Thus exoterism has a certain right to be uninterested in all that does not enter into its own system, or into its *upāya* — its "saving stratagem" — as the Buddhists would say.

It is not without relevance here to point out the existence of an "average" esoterism, unaware of its true nature and based on the idea that on the one hand metaphysics proceeds from theology, and that on the other gnosis proceeds from religious zeal; we would rather say — and this is quite different — that the integral doctrine proceeds from the elementary doctrine and that effective gnosis proceeds from theoretical gnosis. Doubtless, the opinion mentioned above is partly true, for the gnostic does not cease being a man; but quite obviously, the reason for being of his vocation is a virtuality that precisely transcends the human. The spiritual anthropology of authentic esoterism starts from the idea that man is defined by a total and "deiform" intelligence, whereas the common religion readily defines man as "sinner," "slave," even "nothing"; hence in accordance with the "fall" or with creaturely limitation alone, rather than with his inalienable substance or, consequently, with the "divine content."

All the preceding amounts to saying that the human soul possesses two poles: the empirical self, which aspires to salvation and whose vehicle is the will, and the intellect, which tends towards its source, both transcendent and immanent, and whose vehicle is the intelligence.[5] Participation in the intellect comprises several degrees: it can be direct and demanding as with the man of gnosis, and it can be indirect and modest as with the average initiated artisans who follow their "metaphysical instinct," which is within the reach of every really normal man. To carve stone is to render "animic matter" receptive in view of a liberating awakening; at the same time — since one works for a sanctuary — it is to collaborate in the construction of a "new Jerusalem." Moreover, every object that is universally useful — and therefore beautiful of its kind — is a positive symbol and indirectly pertains to the sacred: in making an object according to so to speak "alchemical" rules, the artisan recreates himself starting from the "brute stone" and in view of the ascending path; he repeats, or rather prefigures, inwardly what he does outwardly. Here as in all esoterism, the operative principle is not sentimental humility, it is self-transforming knowledge.[6]

The relationship between sacred art and esoterism is explained by the celestial origin of this art, although the racial or cultural soul participates to a certain extent in the elaboration of styles, as it participates even in the formula-

5. Exoterism readily reduces intelligence to reason alone, and then goes even further in having every concept derive from sensorial experience — this is the sensualist thesis — which allows the exclusive revelationists to deny pure intellection, hence the very principle of the *Sophia Perennis*.

6. As a Hindu text declares: "There is no lustral water like unto Knowledge" *(jnāna)*.

tion of revealed Texts;[7] every theophany is in its way "true God and true man."

*

* *

Having alluded above to sentimental humility, we would here specify the following: it is true that pious "subjectivity," if it is sincere, opens itself to Mercy, but this is not a reason for believing that it alone is efficacious; "objectivity" is also a gift of Heaven, to say the least. Obviously there is nothing to fault in sentiment when it does not usurp the place of intelligence and when on the contrary it is determined by Truth, Beauty, the Good, and without any excess that could diminish their influence.

Sentiment, if it is rightly inspired, is an adequation: it is to love what is lovable, detest what is detestable, admire what is admirable, disdain what is contemptible, fear what is fearful and trust what is trustworthy; the positive quintessence of sentiment being love, which is a divine dimension. From this priority it follows that to detest is not properly speaking to create an aversion, it is rather to withdraw love, which exists before hate, as lovable things exist before detestable things, ontologically speaking; whereas to love is not to withdraw a preexisting hatred — inexistent in fact — it is to remain in the original attitude: in the love that, according to Dante, "moves the sun and the other stars."

*

* *

The *Sophia Perennis* is to know the total Truth and, consequently, to will the Good and love Beauty; and this in conformity to this Truth, hence with full awareness of the

7. This allows of understanding the seriousness of any blow to the traditional arts; the introduction of baroque art for example was one of the great calamities of western Christianity, comparable — at its level — to the falsification of a liturgy or of a canonical text.

reasons for doing so. The doctrinal *Sophia* treats of the Divine Principle on the one hand and of its universal Manifestation on the other: hence of God, the world and the soul, while distinguishing within Manifestation between the macrocosm and the microcosm; this implies that God comprises in Himself — extrinsically at least — degrees and modes, that is to say that He tends to limit Himself in view of His Manifestation. Therein lies all the mystery of the Divine *Māyā*.

To know the Truth, to will the Good, to love Beauty. We have just characterized the element Truth; as for the Good, it is a priori the supreme Principle as quintessence and cause of every possible good; and it is a posteriori on the one hand that which in the Universe manifests the Principle, and on the other hand that which leads back to the Principle; in a word, the Good is first of all God Himself, then the "projection" of God into existence, and finally the "reintegration" of the existentiated into God.[8] Let us specify that for man, the three highest goods are: firstly religion, secondly piety, and thirdly salvation, taking these terms in an almost absolute sense and outside any restrictive specification. As for the goods that do not enter into these three categories, they participate in them either in a direct or in an indirect manner, for every good has the value of a symbol, hence of a key.

As for Beauty, it stems from Infinitude, which coincides with the divine Bliss; seen in this connection, God is Beauty, Love, Goodness and Peace, and He penetrates the whole Universe with these qualities. Beauty, in the Universe, is that which reveals the divine Infinitude: every created beauty communicates to us something infinite, beatific, liberating.[9] Love, which responds to Beauty, is the desire for union, or

8. One will recall this Patristic formula: "God became man that man might become God."

9. No doubt there are also terrible beauties, that of fire or that of the hurricane, or of creatures such as the tiger or the eagle; which means, not

it is union itself; according to Ibn 'Arabi, the way towards God is Love because God is Beauty.

Goodness, for its part, is the generous radiation of Beauty: it is to Beauty what heat is to light. Being Beauty, God is thereby Goodness or Mercy: we could also say that in Beauty, God lends us something of Paradise; the beautiful is the messenger, not only of Infinitude and Harmony, but also, like the rainbow, of reconciliation and pardon. From an altogether different standpoint, Goodness and Beauty are the respectively "inward" and "outward" aspects of Beatitude, whereas from the standpoint of our preceding distinction, Beauty is intrinsic inasmuch as it pertains to the Essence, whereas Goodness is extrinsic inasmuch as it is exercised in relation to accidents, namely towards creatures.

In this dimension, Rigor, which stems from the Absolute, could not be absent: intrinsically, it is the adamantine purity of the divine and of the sacred; extrinsically, it is the limitation of pardon, owing to the lack of receptivity of given creatures. The world is woven of two major dimensions, mathematical rigor and musical gentleness; both are united in a superior homogeneity that pertains to the very fathomlessness of the Divinity.

In such truths or mysteries, the exoteric and esoteric perspectives — religions and wisdoms — participate in accordance with their capabilities and their vocations: esoterism in considering strictly the nature of things, and exoterism in filtering and adapting it to human opportunities, while conveying behind this veil the treasures of the one and unanimous *Sophia*. In the very depths of certain men there always resides, intact, man as such; and consequently also the plenary knowledge of God.

that beauty is terrible in itself, but that the terrible can participate in beauty; and this because it can be noble, that is to say in conformity with a heavenly archetype.

*

* *

What defines man is that of which he alone is capable: namely total intelligence — endowed with objectivity and transcendence — free will, and generous character; or quite simply objectivity, hence adequation of the will and of sentiment as well as of intelligence. The *Sophia Perennis* is, basically, objectivity freed from all shackles: it is the capacity to "perceive" that which is, to the point of being able to "be" that which is; it is the capacity to conform to necessary — not only possible — Being.

The animal cannot leave his state, whereas man can; strictly speaking, only he who is fully man can leave the closed system of the individuality, through participation in the one and universal Selfhood. There lies the mystery of the human vocation: what man "can," he "must"; on this plane, to be able to is to have to, given that the capacity pertains to a positive substance. Or again, which fundamentally amounts to the same thing: to know is to be; to know That which is, and That which alone is.

The Twofold Discernment

There are two discernments, that of principles and that of facts. The first is the intuition of metaphysical realities, the second applies to phenomena. One the one hand, this second discernment is the sense of proportions and hence of priorities, and on the other, it is the sense of causality; the first relationship pertains to "space" — abstract as well as concrete — and the second relationship more to "time." To have the sense of proportions is, among other things, to see small things in relation to the large and never to isolate them totally from their principial context whether near or remote; to have the sense of causality is to know how to draw consequences, thus it is to see effects in causes and causes in effects; all this being the very definition of intelligence.

In human intelligence there is something supernatural, which amounts to saying, paradoxically but profoundly, that the supernatural is natural to man.[1]

*

* *

1. This observation allows one to gauge to what extent the loss of religion is a disaster for a human society; it is to deprive man of a vital substance and to dehumanize him. All the reasonings in the world cannot replace that apparently irrational, but in fact suprarational and profoundly realistic, element which is religion.

A prince gave a palace to Ibn 'Arabi, who shortly thereafter gave it to a beggar. From the standpoint of reason, this is absurd in several respects — for the prince as well as for the saint and the poor man — but from the standpoint of noumenal and symbolist discernment this can and must have a meaning.

We have said that there are two kinds of discernment, the first situated on the plane of metaphysical realities, and the second, on that of earthly phenomena; now it is far from the case that both these discernments are always realized to the same degree, despite the adage that "he who is capable of the greater is capable of the lesser," which is true in principle and from the standpoint of potentialities, but not necessarily from that of effective capacities. Unquestionably, a situation demonstrated by many examples is the imbalance — or inequality — between intrinsic discernment, that of principles, and extrinsic discernment, that of facts: the latter are then considered not in themselves but as symbols, and in this respect, the discernment will not lack pertinence. Thus on the plane of earthly phenomena, we can distinguish between a direct, concrete, effective discernment of things, and an indirect, abstract, noumenal and symbolist discernment; many "holy absurdities" are explained thereby. When Ibn 'Arabi gave a poor man a luxurious home, he saw only the principial aspect of the situation, namely the vanity of riches and the beauty of generosity; the world then appeared to him as a great book containing only principles and archetypes. But there is something else: it is no doubt necessary here to take into consideration the desire on the part of saints to always give a good example, and also the quasi-sacrificial intention to compensate, by spectacular exaggerations, the innumerable sins of the world of mediocrity; which also explains why Ibn 'Arabi took the trouble to immortalize the incident in one of his books, it being out of the question to suspect him of the least vanity.

Keeping to the standpoint of the priority accorded to the "ideal" or to the "noumenal," we will also mention the following incident: the Prophet possessed, near Medina, the oasis of Fadak; after his death, his daughter Fatimah expected to inherit it, but the caliph Abu Bakr was opposed to this and argued that according to Islamic law "prophets have no heirs." Now one may suppose, without the risk of being mistaken, that for Fatimah this oasis was like an earthly reflection of her father and like a ray of Paradise; thus it was a treasure exempt from ordinary legal rules, whereas for Abu Bakr on the contrary, the oasis was merely a profane property, subject to the rules of the Law. Here we see the clash between two perspectives, the "vertical" and the "horizontal," or the symbolist and the legalist.

To return to holy excesses: some people will perhaps tell us that the gift of a castle to a beggar is an absurdity and that practical discernment, in short good sense, requires no extraordinary gift. Now it is plain as day that the average man is lacking in discernment, as is shown particularly by politicians, and by the crowds who approve them; not to mention the almost total lack of discernment in the philosophical, cultural, psychological, aesthetic and other domains. If "good sense" sufficed to resolve all real or apparent problems, there would be no need to complain here-below; clearly, those saints who sin through excess of symbolism or through expeditious zeal have, on many a crucial point, much more realistic opinions than "reasonable" but spiritually insignificant men. As we have written more than once, to be perfectly objective is to die a little; the average man is certainly not ready to consent to that.

*

* *

In traditional civilizations and before the modern age, phenomenal discernment regarding sensible forms was so to speak in the air, so that critical sense or "good taste" was not as urgent as it is in the universe of modernism. It was the entire tradition which "thought" for man, the sense of harmony was everywhere, it emanated supernaturally from the tradition itself; traditional art pertains indirectly, but concretely, to Revelation, which moreover allows one to understand the significance of craft initiations. And it also explains that paradoxical phenomenon of the rarity of formal discernment, and even of phenomenal discernment pure and simple, in contemporary traditional milieus; this in worlds that, being in principle capable of the "greater," should also be capable of the "lesser." What is lacking here is a discipline of the "sensorial" and aesthetic intelligence, the roots of which necessarily go deep into noumenal intelligence; intelligence as such being open to all the knowable and having a priori no right to infirmities. However, it is appropriate to distinguish between an intelligence particularly apt for a given, not indispensable, science, and an intelligence open to an essential element of the real, such as beauty, which concerns all men.

Phenomenal discernment comprises at once an analysis and a synthesis: an intellectual and discriminative cognition on the one hand, and an existential and unitive one on the other; in simplified language, we would say that man does not merely discern with his "brain," but also with his "heart." Besides, a man is prone to seeing the archetypes to the extent that he is noble; if he lacks nobleness, he on the contrary clings to the accidental or to the shells, all the more so in that the need to admire is foreign to the nature of the hylic.

It is to phenomenal discernment that the Hindu *darshan* pertains, the visual union with a phenomenon of holiness or even with any phenomenon of beauty insofar as it is viewed in relation to its archetype.

*

* *

If on the one hand the symbolist mentality interprets facts as symbols, on the other hand it can present symbols as facts, many examples of which are offered by the sacred Scriptures; one of the sources of the symbolist mentality is in fact the language of Revelation itself, which is far less interested in the exactitude of phenomena than in their spiritual meaning and in the moral and mystical efficacy of the images. As for the strictly subjective cause of this mentality, it pertains to the psychological order: intense preoccupation with spiritual reality quite naturally entails a certain indifference to the things of this world, and also a tendency to see things only with respect to their principial and universal significations.

Thus the symbolist mentality can be a unilateral tendency of the intelligence and the sensibility, but it can also be a spiritual realism on the plane of phenomena, in which case it gives rise to a sanctity based, not on negation, rejection and sacrifice, but on the concrete analogy between earthly phenomena and heavenly archetypes.[2] This is the distinction between a Shankara and an Abhinavagupta or a Krishna, or between a Desert Father and David or Solomon; what is involved is not the cosmic scope of the holy personages,[3] but only their manner of combining their already heavenly station with the phenomena of earthly life. The ascetics turn away from creatures because creatures are not God; others on the contrary have the capacity to accept creatures because they manifest Him, and to the extent that they do so, this being the perspective of tantrism. There lies the whole difference between the accidents and the substance: between a particular beauty and beauty as such; or between the reflection as such and the phenomenon as reflected principle. If it is true that we bear within ourselves what we love without, it is equally true that we meet without what we bear

2. "This universe is woven in thy being (O Shiva), but it is also projected outwardly. I have understood this at the cost of many efforts; may I also realize it through the experience of the senses." (*Shivastotravālī,* by Utpaladeva, a Shivite of Kashmir of the 10th century.)

3. The terms *avatāra* and *bodhisattva* comprise fundamental gradations, but it is here only a question of spiritual types and not of theophanic degrees.

within; we love that which we must be, and we must be it because, more deeply and eternally, that is what we are. On the one hand, *Māyā* is *Māyā* and *Ātmā* is *Ātmā;* on the other hand, *Māyā* is "none other" than *Ātmā,* otherwise it would not be.

The Guénonian theory of "descending realization" may come to mind here: whereas — in Buddhist language — the *pratyēka-buddha* has the experience of the ascending way only and has realized *bodhi* solely "for himself," the *bodhisattva* on the contrary has "descended" to the world, and thus has realized *bodhi* also "for others," and for that reason has been invested with a mission. However, we do not believe — even though mahayanic exoterism suggests it — that the station of the *pratyēka-buddha* is "lacking" an essential element nor that there exists a spiritual degree that intrinsically would imply a heavenly mandate;[4] a "redescending" realization can only be an application of an a priori metaphysical discernment to the world of contingencies; it is to take account, not of simple analogies, but of the exact nature of things on the very level of existence. It is in short the perfect balance between the inward and outward domains; it is really "to see God everywhere," not merely beyond the world, but also in the structure of the world itself. Things have the right to be what they are, and one must know how to take them for what they are, which could not exclude, in one and the same subject, the parallel or simultaneous consciousness of archetypes and principles, thus the symbolist perspective inasmuch as it represents a norm and an equilibrium.

*

*   *

Specifically human intelligence is in principle the capability to know all the knowable, so much so that there is

4. This means that in the life of a spiritual man the fact of a mission does not necessarily coincide with the supreme station — *bodhi* — nor for that matter with perfect discernment within the phenomenal order.

nothing real that cannot be discerned by man; no doubt there is an indefinite multitude of facts beyond our reach, de facto if not de jure; but truth, to the extent that it is important and that it contains and illumines all contingencies, is immanent in our spirit and is manifested therein in accordance with our receptivity: with our conformity to the nature of That which is.

As Muhammad Al-Harraq[5] said in his *Dīwān:* "Seekest thou Layla, when she is manifest in thee, and believest thou her to be other, when she is none other than thee?" But man is so made that this Layla is accessible only in virtue of exterior factors of divine origin, beginning with Revelation, which precisely is not other than an objectification of our immanent Knowledge.

5. A Sufi of Tetuan of the 19th century.

Part Three

Moral and Spiritual Dimensions

Cosmic Shadows and Serenity

"God doeth what He wills": this means, not that God, like an individual, could have arbitrary desires, but that pure Being by its very nature comprises All-Possibility; now the limitlessness of All-Possibility implies possibilities that are so to speak absurd, that is to say contrary to the nature of Being, which every phenomenon is yet supposed to manifest, and does so whether it likes it or not. Obviously these possibilities can be realized only in illusory and circumscribed mode, for no evil could penetrate the celestial order. Evil, far from constituting half of possibility — there is no symmetry between good and evil — is limited by space and time to the point of being reduced to an infinitesimal quantity in the economy of the total Universe; it is necessarily thus because "Mercy embraceth all things"; and *vincit omnia Veritas.*

In other words: divine Infinitude implies that the supreme Principle consents, not only to limit itself ontologically — by degrees and in view of universal Manifestation — but also to be contradicted within Manifestation itself. Every metaphysician admits this intellectually, but it is far from the case that every one accepts it to the same extent morally, that is to say, by being resigned to the concrete consequences of the principle of necessary absurdity.

In order to resolve the thorny problem of evil, some have claimed that nothing is evil because everything that happens is "willed by God," or that evil exists only from the "standpoint of the Law." This is unacceptable, firstly because it is God who lays down the Law, and secondly because the Law exists on account of evil and not vice versa. What should be said is that evil is integrated within the universal Good, not as evil but as an ontological necessity; this necessity underlies evil, it is metaphysically inherent in it, yet without thereby transforming it into a good.

Thus one must not say that God "wills" evil — let us rather say that He "allows" it — nor that evil is a good because God is not against its existence; however, one may say that we must accept God's will when evil enters into our destiny and when it is not possible for us to avoid it, or as long as it is not possible. Moreover, let us not forget that the complement of resignation is trust, the quintessence of which is the certitude at once metaphysical and eschatological that we bear deep within us — the unconditional certitude of That which is, and the conditional certitude of that which we can be.

*
* *

Evil participates in the good in various ways; first by its existence inasmuch as this existence manifests Being, hence the Sovereign Good; second, and on the contrary, by its disappearance, for victory over evil is a good and is not possible without the presence of an evil; third, evil can participate in the good as an instrument, for it can happen that an evil collaborates in the production of a good; fourth, this participation may consist in the accentuation of a good by the contrast between it and its opposite. Finally, negative or privative phenomena manifest God's "capability" to contradict Himself as it were, and this possibility is required by the very perfection of Being; but, as Meister Eckhardt said, "the more he blasphemes the more he praises God." Moreover, it can happen that good and evil are mingled, whence the possibility of a "lesser evil"; this coincides with the very notion of relativity. As for the question of knowing why a possibility is possible, that is either unanswerable, or else it is resolved in advance by the axiom of All-Possibility immanent in Being, and which by definition is without limits; quite paradoxically, it can be said that All-Possibility would not be what it is if it did not realize impossibility in a certain fashion.

Absolute Reality — Beyond Being, *Paramātmā* — has no opposite; but Being, the personal God, comprises an opposite because Being is comprised in universal Relativity, *Māyā*, of which it is the summit. This opposite, Satan, could not however be situated on the same level as God, so that God too can be said to "have no opposite," at least in a certain — but essential — respect; thus God is "in Heaven" *(en tois ouranois)*, whereas the devil, and with him hell, pertains to the sub-celestial world. Be that as it may, the satanic possibility is given, ontologically speaking, by relativity itself, which requires not only gradations but also oppositions; relativity is basically the movement towards nothingness, which possesses a shadow of reality only because of this movement; all this, we repeat, in virtue of the infinitude of Being.

A distinction analogous to the one that we have just raised is the opposition between spirit and matter, with the difference that the latter is neutral and not malefic; nonetheless the distinction between the "spirit" and the "flesh" identifies the latter in practice with evil — for reasons of moral and mystical opportuneness — losing sight of the metaphysical transparency of phenomena in general and of sensations in particular, hence their principial ambiguity and neutrality.[1] In other words, and to be more precise: if matter as such is neutral — nothing is more pure than a crystal — there is however a disgrace in its combination with

1. It goes without saying that theology, which admits "sensible consolations," is not strictly Manichean, that is, it does not forget the divine origin of the bodily substance; Christ and the Blessed Virgin had bodies, and these bodies rose up to Heaven; no doubt they were transfigured, but they did not lose their bodily nature.

life, whence impurity, sickness and death; a relative disgrace that does not preclude interferences of the celestial into terrestrial life. Geometrically and analogically speaking, decay is possible in the concentric circles, but the rays originating from the center and traversing them remain incorruptible; this principle applies not only to the ambiguity of matter, but also to the excess of contingencies in which we are obliged to live, and which only our relationship with Heaven can manage to compensate and vanquish.

But not only is there the grip of matter on the spirit, of outwardness on inwardness, of dispersion on concentration, there is also the predominance of psychism over the intelligence, and this flaw — which could never be corrected by a superficial rationality — even succeeds in compromising victories over matter; although Heaven may also use this infirmity for its ends and in such cases remove the moral harmfulness of it; one of the generosities of Mercy is to take men as they are, to the extent possible.[2]

*

* *

We have said above: it is necessary to accept "God's will" when evil enters into our destiny and cannot possibly be avoided; indeed, the partially paradoxical nature of All-Possibility requires of man an attitude of conformity to this situation, namely the quality of serenity, of which the sky above us is the visible sign. Serenity is to keep oneself so to speak above the clouds, in the calm and coolness of emptiness and far from all the dissonances of this lower world; it is never to allow the soul to immerse itself in impasses of disturbances, bitterness, or secret revolt, for it is necessary to beware of implicitly accusing Being when accusing some phenomenon. We do not say that one should not accuse evil

2. We have in mind here not only the Semitic monotheistic religions, but also certain sectors in Hinduism and in Buddhism.

in all justice, we say that one should not accuse it with an attitude of despair, losing sight of the everywhere-present Sovereign Good and, in another respect, of the imperatives of universal equilibrium; the world is what it must be.

Serenity is resignation, at once intellectual and moral, to the nature of things: it is patience in relation to All-Possibility insofar as the latter requires, by its very limitlessness, the existence of negative possibilities, those that deny Being and the qualities manifesting It, as we have noted above. We would also say, in order to provide one more key, that serenity consists in resigning oneself to that destiny, at once unique and permanent, which is the present moment: to this itinerant "now" that no one can avoid and that in its substance pertains to the Eternal. The man who is conscious of the nature of pure Being willingly remains in the moment that Heaven has assigned him; he is not feverishly straining towards the future nor lovingly or sadly bent over the past. The pure present is the moment of the Absolute: it is now — neither yesterday nor tomorrow — that we stand before God.

The quality of serenity evokes that of dignity: far from being merely a matter of outward demeanor, natural and sincere dignity has a spiritual basis, namely the quasi-existential awareness of the "prime mover"; the man who is concretely aware of greatnesses that surpass him could not disavow them in his behavior, and this is moreover what his deiformity demands; in fact, there is no piety without dignity. Man's reason for being is to be situated above the plane of existence upon which he has been projected, or upon which, in a certain respect, he has projected himself; and this while adapting himself to the nature of that plane. Man's cosmic mission is to be *pontifex*, "bridge-builder": of the path that links the sensible and moving world to the immutable divine Shore.

*

* *

Thus serenity is the quasi-unconditional moral victory either over the natural shadows, or over the absurd dissonances of the world and of life; in the case of encounters with evil — and we owe it to God and to ourselves to remain in Peace — we may use the following arguments. First, no evil can take anything away from the Sovereign Good or ought to disturb our relationship with God; we must never lose sight of absolute values when in contact with the absurd. Second, we must be conscious of the metaphysical necessity of evil; "it must needs be that offences come." Third, let us not lose sight of the limits or the relativity of evil; for God shall have the last word. Fourth, it is clearly necessary to be resigned to God's will, that is, to our destiny; destiny, by definition, is what we cannot but encounter, and thus it is an aspect of ourselves. Fifth — and this follows from the preceding argument — God wishes to try our faith, hence also our sincerity and our patience, not to mention our gratitude; this is why one speaks of the "trials of life." Sixth, God will not ask us to account for what others do, nor for what happens to us without our being directly responsible for it; He will only ask us to account for what we are directly responsible for; He will only ask us to account for what we ourselves do. Seventh and last, pure happiness is not for this life, it is for the next; perfection is not of this world, but this world is not everything, and the last word belongs to Beatitude.

Virtue and Way

The first of the virtues is veracity, for without truth we can do nothing. The second virtue is sincerity, which consists in drawing the consequences of what we know to be true, and which implies all the other virtues; for it is not enough to acknowledge the truth objectively, in thought, it must also be assumed subjectively, in acts, whether outward or inward. Truth excludes heedlessness and hypocrisy as much as error and lying.

Sincerity implies two initial concrete attitudes: abstention from what is contrary to truth, and accomplishment of what is in conformity to it; in other words, it is necessary to abstain from all that draws one away from the Sovereign Good — which coincides with the Real — and to accomplish all that brings us closer to it. This is why to the virtues of veracity and sincerity are added those of temperance and fervor, or of purity and vigilance, and also, even more fundamentally, those of humility and charity.

Without virtue there is no Way, no matter what the worth of our spiritual means may be; virtue, directly, is sincerity, and indirectly, veracity. Virtue is not a merit in itself, it is a gift; but it is nonetheless a merit to the extent that we exert ourselves towards it.

*

*   *

I and others: the moral qualities that correspond respectively to these two dimensions of our existence are effacement and generosity; or in other words, humility and charity, not as a priori sentimental attitudes but as moral and spiritual adaptations to the nature of things.

The quintessential foundation of the virtue of effacement or humility is that man is not God, or that the human "I" is not the Divine "Self"; and the foundation of the virtue of generosity, of compassion or of charity is that our neighbor too is "made in the image of God," or that the Divine Self is immanent in every human subject. It is this deiformity that likewise explains the quality of dignity, which moreover results from our capacity — deiform as well — to participate in the Divine Majesty through our awareness of it.

Effacement and generosity: on the one hand, one must efface oneself with dignity; on the other hand, one has to be generous with measure, for the interests of others do not abolish our own interests, and besides, not all men have the right to the same consideration, except in the quite general respect of the human condition. Moreover, charity does not necessarily offer what is immediately agreeable, otherwise there would be no bitter remedy; to punish a child justly is more charitable than to spoil him. To think otherwise would amount to abolishing all justice and all moral and social health.

The question of the balance between effacement and dignity calls forth the following specification: while recognizing that the creature is a nothingness in relation to God, we must not lose sight of the fact that God has willed the existence of the creature and that in this respect it can possess a certain greatness in the world that is its own; it does not possess this greatness merely in its cosmic ambiance, it has it also, and a priori, in the Divine Intellect itself, since in creating a given being God wished to create a given greatness. The same holds true for freedom, to add only this particularly controversial example: to the argument that God alone is free and that all else is predestined, we reply that nonetheless, in creating free beings, God wished to manifest freedom and nothing else, and that consequently beings are really free with respect to this divine intention. The mode or degree of cosmic manifestation implies limitations — the mere fact of manifestation already implies them — but the content of this projection nevertheless remains identical to what constitutes its reason for being.

For pious sentimentality, humility means that man not be aware of his worth, as if intelligence were not capable of objectivity with respect to this phenomenal order that is the human soul; it is precisely this objectivity which implies that the fully intelligent man be aware also of the relativity of his gifts, his qualities, his merits.

Clearly, the quintessence of humility, we insist, is the awareness of our nothingness in the face of the Absolute; in the same order of ideas, the quintessence of charity is our love of the Sovereign Good, which gives to our social compassion its most profound meaning. Indeed, not to love God is to deny Him, and to deny Him is ipso facto to deny the immortality of the soul and consequently the meaning of life, which takes away from our beneficence if not all its meaning at least the greater part of it; for charity towards the strictly earthly man — the human animal if one will — must be accompanied by charity towards the virtually celestial man, all the more so in that purely "horizontal" charity can be combined with the murder of a soul, whereas a suffering that is shared by no one else can be a good for the immortal soul.[1] Let this be said, not in order to discourage intentions of charity of course, but in order to recall that for

1. There is also, obligatorily, charity towards animals, but in this case the question of spiritual duty to an immortal soul does not arise. One cannot give to an animal more than it can receive, but one gives it what it can receive because, at its level, it is our neighbor; all this is independent of the fact that an animal can be penetrated by a *barakah,* that it can be the vehicle of a spiritual influence.

man every value must refer to the Sovereign Good, on pain of remaining a two-edged sword.

*

* *

All virtue has its aspect of beauty, which renders it immediately lovable, independently of the aspect of usefulness or opportuneness. The combination of effacement and generosity, or of humility and charity, or of modesty and compassion — this combination, which in fact is consubstantial, constitutes virtue as such and therefore the spiritual qualification *sine qua non.* It will perhaps be objected that if such is the case, no one is fully qualified for spirituality; now part of virtue is the intention to realize it, so that essential virtue is at once a condition and a result. God does not at the outset ask perfection of us, but He does ask of us its intention, which implies, if it is sincere, the absence of serious imperfections; it is only too obvious that a proud man cannot aspire sincerely to humility. God asks of us that which He has given us, namely the qualities we bear in our own depths, in our deiform substance; man must "become what he is"; every being is fundamentally Being as such.

On Love

The love of God results necessarily from the logic of things: to love the accidents is to love the Substance, unconsciously or consciously. The spiritual man may love things or creatures which in themselves are not God, but he cannot love them without God or outside Him; thus they bring him back towards the Sovereign Good in a quasi-sacramental manner, while they themselves are only what they are. "It is not for the love of the husband that the husband is dear, but for the love of *Ātmā* that is in him": by directly loving a creature, we indirectly love the Creator, necessarily so because "every thing is *Ātmā.*" Nobleness of love is, on the part of the subject, to choose the object that is worthy of love and to love it without avidity or tyranny, while being aware — quasi-existentially — of its heavenly archetype and of its divine substance; as for the object worthy of love, it ennobles him who loves it, to the extent that it is loved in God. What is pure, primordial and thereby normatively human, has its roots in the divine order and tends ipso facto towards its own Origin.

To say love is to say beauty; the aspect of beauty, in God, is of primary importance in the context of spiritual love. Love implies the desire of possession and of union; in this direct sense, to love God is, if not to wish to possess Him, at least to wish to experience His Presence and His Grace, and in the final analysis to desire to be united with Him, to the extent that our spiritual potentiality and our destiny allow.

Love's object is beauty, as we have said; now God's Beauty stems from His Infinitude, which coincides with His Bliss and His tendency to communicate it, hence to radiate; this is the "overflowing" of the Sovereign Good, which at one and the same time projects its beauties and attracts souls. The Infinite makes itself present to us and at the same time frees us from ourselves; not by destroying us, but on the contrary by leading us to what we are in our immortal essence.

One may speak of beauty only on condition of knowing that it is a perfectly objective reality, independent of the subjective factors of affinity or taste; the appreciation of beauty is firstly a matter of comprehension and then a matter of sensitivity. That is beautiful which, in the world of expressions, is in conformity with its own heavenly essence, this being the reason for its existence; in God Himself, the hypostatic "expression" of the Essence is Beatitude, *Ānanda;* it is this latter which in the final analysis is the foundation of all beauty. And Beatitude coincides with the divine "Dimension" of Infinitude, in virtue of which God shows Himself as the Sovereign Good, source of all harmony and all happiness.

*
* *

There is a love of God that constitutes a method and whose starting point is a theology, and there is another love of God whose starting point is knowledge of the divine Nature and consequently the sense of the divine Beauty, which frees us from the narrowness and the din of the terrestrial world. The way of love — methodical *bhakti* — presupposes that through it alone can we go towards God; whereas love as such — intrinsic *bhakti* — accompanies the way of knowledge, *jnāna,* and is based essentially on our sensitivity to the divine Beauty. It is from this quasi-Platonic perspective that sacred art derives, and that is why this art always pertains to the domain of esoterism; *ars sine scientia nihil.*

Consequently it is important to understand that the metaphysical and so to speak abstract aspects of God also suggest beauties and reasons for love; the contemplative soul may be sensitive to the immense serenity proper to pure Being, or to the lightning-like crystallinity of the Absolute; or one may — aside from other aspects — love God for what is adamantine in His immutability, or for what is warm and liberating in His Infinitude. In our terrestrial world there are sensible beauties: those of the limitless sky, of the radiant sun, of lightning, of the crystal; all these beauties reflect something of God. Moral beauties are analogically of the same order; one may love the virtues for their so to speak aesthetic participation in the beauties of divine Being, just as one may and ought to love them for their specific and immediate values.

Beauty, love, happiness: man yearns for happiness because Beatitude, which is made of beauty and love, is his very substance. "All my thoughts speak of love," said Dante in a sense at once terrestrial and celestial.

Tutti i miei pensier parlan d'amore.

BY THE SAME AUTHOR

The Transcendent Unity of Religions, *Faber and Faber, 1953*
Revised Edition, *Harper & Row, 1974*
The Theosophical Publishing House, 1984

Spiritual Perspectives and Human Facts, *Faber and Faber, 1954*
Perennial Books, 1969
New Translation, *Perennial Books, 1987*

Language of the Self, *Ganesh, 1959*

Gnosis: Divine Wisdom, *John Murray, 1959*
Perennial Books, 1990

Stations of Wisdom, *John Murray, 1961*
Perennial Books, 1980

Understanding Islam, *Allen and Unwin, 1963, 1965, 1976, 1979, 1981*
Penguin Books, 1972

Light on the Ancient Worlds, *Perennial Books, 1966*
World Wisdom Books, 1984

In the Tracks of Buddhism, *Allen and Unwin, 1968*
Unwin-Hyman, 1989

Dimensions of Islam, *Allen and Unwin, 1969*

Logic and Transcendence, *Harper and Row, 1975*
Perennial Books, 1984

Esoterism as Principle and as Way, *Perennial Books, 1981*

Castes and Races, *Perennial Books, 1981*

Sufism: Veil and Quintessence, *World Wisdom Books, 1981*

From the Divine to the Human, *World Wisdom Books, 1982*

Christianity/Islam: Essays on Esoteric Ecumenicism,
World Wisdom Books, 1985

The Essential Writings of Frithjof Schuon (S. H. Nasr, Ed.)
Amity House, 1986

Survey of Metaphysics and Esoterism, *World Wisdom Books, 1986*

In the Face of the Absolute, *World Wisdom Books, 1989*

The Feathered Sun: Plains Indians in Art & Philosophy,
World Wisdom Books, 1990

To Have a Center, *World Wisdom Books, 1990*

Pearls of the Pilgrim, *World Wisdom Books, in preparation*

Images of Primordial & Mystic Beauty:
Paintings by Frithjof Schuon,
Abodes, in preparation

INDEX

Index

Index

Index